Microsoft® Windows® 98

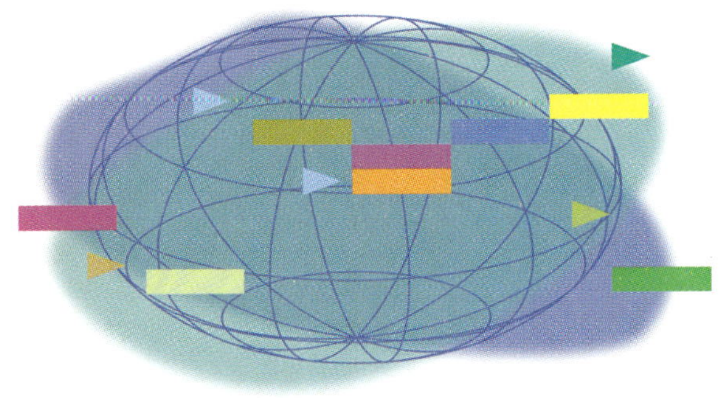

Tim Duffy

Prentice Hall
Upper Saddle River
New Jersey 07458

To Wendy and Michael,
the two most important people in my life

Editor-in-Chief: Mickey Cox
Executive Editor: Alex von Rosenberg
Acquisitions Editor: Anita Devine
Editorial Assistant: Jennifer Surich
Marketing Manager: Kris King
Managing Editor: Deanna Storey
Project Manager: Lynne Breitfeller
Project Management and Text Design: Elm Street Publishing Services, Inc.
Senior Manufacturing Supervisor: Paul Smolenski
Manufacturing Manager: Vincent Scelta
Production Manager: Gail Steier de Acevedo
Design Manager: Patricia Smythe
Interior Design: Brian Salisbury
Cover Design: Joan Connor
Cover Illustration: Brian Salisbury
Composition: Gillian Hall, The Aardvark Group

0-201-45910-8

Prentice-Hall International (UK) Limited, London
Prentice-Hall of Australia Pty. Limited, Sydney
Prentice-Hall Canada, Inc., Toronto
Prentice-Hall Hispanoamericana, S.A., Mexico
Prentice-Hall of India Private Limited, New Delhi
Prentice-Hall of Japan, Inc., Tokyo
Editora Prentice-Hall do Brasil, Ltda., Rio de Janeiro

Printed in the United States of America

10 9 8 7 6 5 4 3 2

Microsoft® Windows® 98

CONTENTS

PREFACE

Welcome to *Microsoft® Windows® 98* by Tim Duffy.

NEW TO MICROSOFT® WINDOWS® 98

New Text Design. As you open the pages of *Microsoft® Windows® 98,* you will immediately notice the clear, easy-to-follow interior design. The clean page layout includes ample white space for notetaking and a wealth of visual aids to guide students through each project.

Web Tools. Connectivity is paramount in computing and business. Today's students are required, more than ever, to know how to use the World Wide Web and Web development tools. *Microsoft® Windows® 98* by Tim Duffy has changed with the technology. It features all the latest in Microsoft® Office Web development and connectivity tools including Internet Explorer 5, Outlook® 2000, FrontPage® 2000, and the Web-integrated operating system of Windows® 98.

Interdisciplinary Exercises. Learning Microsoft® Office applications does not happen in a vacuum. In addition to learning the fundamentals of each application, students must also be able to take their experience using software applications and apply it to their other courses and experiences. In addition to the wealth of business-oriented exercises in this book, Tim Duffy has added interdisciplinary exercises that show students how to use software applications in other fields as well as for personal use.

AN AUTHOR YOU CAN COUNT ON

For more than two decades, Tim Duffy has been teaching and writing. As a teacher, he has taught introductory computer courses to thousands of Illinois State University students. As an author, he has introduced the very same computing concepts and skills to millions of students worldwide through his highly successful series.

In both his classes and his books, Duffy achieves a perfect balance between concept and skill—the why and the how—of computing. The "why" is the foundation of computing. Learn the concept and why that concept is important, and you can implement any skill. Because he teaches introductory computing throughout the school year, Duffy knows first-hand the conceptual information and techniques students need and want to learn and the best way to present the material. Duffy knows what works in the classroom and what works in the computer labs. He knows where students have difficulty and designs his book to help present concepts clearly. He has developed examples, assignments, and exercises that illuminate concepts and uses techniques to teach each application effectively.

Duffy teaches what he writes and writes what he teaches. In his books, he brings his classroom teaching experience directly to you with the most innovative, up-to-date material available anywhere. His pedagogy is classroom-tried and tested.

BUILDING KNOWLEDGE

For Duffy, learning is like building knowledge. A concept is presented, a feature or task is briefly described, and then students work with it. They complete an exercise or practice a task. Once that task is learned, they add a little more, building on what they are learning. After completing a small group of such tasks, each within its own context, students are presented with projects that unify concepts and skills. To achieve this natural balance between concepts and skills, there is constant reinforcement and evaluation throughout the book, including:

- *Unifying Features.* **Common Features of Office 2000** applications and tasks/features common to those applications give students an overview of how to use an integrated suite.
- *Active Learning.* **Hands-On Exercises** apply software commands and features of each Office 2000 application program to a specific problem, reinforcing skills described in the text.
- **Running Case.** Everyday problems are presented with just enough information to challenge the students. The Running Case teaches critical thinking while reinforcing the basic skills that students have learned to that point.
- **Document to Web Presentation.** This shows students how to transform an ordinary document into a professional presentation. They will be effectively guided through the process of enhancing the original, putting it on the Web, and then, finally, improving the Web page so as to produce a professional electronic document.
- *Task Steps and Reference.* **Reinforcing the Exercise** sections provide students with summary information on how a task is performed to reinforce learning and to provide a reference for the future.
- *Self-Learning.* **On Your Own** boxes allow students to gain additional mastery of features as they explore Office 2000 applications on their own.
- **Timely Tips.** Special notations tell students what potential traps they may encounter with a software tool, what can go wrong, and how to remedy the problem, as well as provide helpful hints on how to use a particular software feature.
- **Toolbar Button Reference.** Tables of toolbar buttons give students a central location to find summaries of buttons found on frequently used toolbars.
- **Keyboard and Toolbar Icons.** Task-specific icons appear frequently in headings and tables to help students identify and remember keystrokes or toolbar buttons required for accessing a particular software feature or performing a particular task.
- *Self-Evaluation.* **End-of-session exercises** offer reinforcement in multiple formats including true/false, multiple choice, short answer, and project-based questions.
- *Web Integration.* Web-based exercises appear at the end of each session in the **Internet Exercises** section. The Web site provides an interactive experience for students as they complete exercises in the text that send them to the site for information or files. In the Web exercises, Duffy teaches students how to view and save graphics, how to navigate on the Web, and how to download files; he even offers a guide to buying a personal computer and help on creating personal home pages.

Duffy takes advantage of the **Web-aware** tools provided with Office 2000 to help students translate their skills for use with the Internet and the Web.

Timely Tips inform students of helpful shortcuts, potential mistakes, or troubleshooting measures they can use with the text.

Interdisciplinary Exercises show students how to use software applications in other fields, such as social sciences, health sciences, and chemistry.

16 Windows 98

Reinforcing the Exercise

1. The Start button is the starting point for all Windows programs, documents, and settings.
2. When you open a window, an application button icon appears in the taskbar.
3. Documents you delete are stored in the Recycle Bin.
4. The My Computer window gives you information on the various resources of the computer, such as disk drives and printers.

CONTROLLING THE DESKTOP APPEARANCE

If your desktop looks different from that depicted so far in this text, your desktop has probably been configured differently. Windows 98 provides much more control over how your desktop appears and how you interact with that desktop. Windows now refers to the desktop as the **Active Desktop**. Certain features, like the appearance of the Internet Explorer Channel Bar, are automatically installed and included when Windows 98 is initially installed. Other features of the Active Desktop have to be specifically selected.

DISPLAYING THE INTERNET EXPLORER CHANNEL BAR

The Internet Explorer Channel Bar appears in its own window when it is active. As a result, you can close the window by clicking the Close button in the upper right-hand corner of that window. The Close button appears when you position the mouse to the top of the Channel Bar. Use the commands in the following Hands-On exercise to redisplay the Channel Bar.

WEB OPTIONS

You can also make your desktop function like World Wide Web applications. This means that each object appears underlined, like an HTML hyperlink, and can be accessed by just clicking the mouse. Web options can be applied using the Folder Options dialog box shown later in Figure 1.23.

HANDS-ON EXERCISE: MANIPULATING THE CHANNEL BAR

1. Close the Channel Bar.

Position the mouse to the top of the Channel Bar (if it is present) and click the Close button of the Internet Explorer Channel Bar.

2. Activate the Channel Bar.

Right-click Right-click a blank area of the Desktop to invoke the context menu.

Active Desktop Choose Active Desktop from the context menu (Figure 1.17).

Customize my Desktop Click on this option to invoke the Display Properties dialog box (Figure 1.18). The dialog box should appear with the Web tab active and the two options shown in Figure 1.18 selected. (If the options

Relating Tables, Modifying Table Structures, and Generating Reports 117

3. Use the Relationships command to relate the Paymast and Paytrans tables. Make certain that you specify referential integrity. Once the relationship is established, access the Paymast table. You should be able to access the corresponding Paytrans records using a subdatasheet.

Interdisciplinary Exercises

The following exercises require the Races and Movies databases used in Session I.

1. Open the Movies Database.
   - a. Link the movies, actors, and directors tables.
   - b. Open the Movies table.
   - c. Add a field named MoneyGrossed, type currency, 0 decimals.
   - d. Add an amount for each movie in the table. (If possible use real data).
   - e. Make the default movietype "Comedy."
   - f. Require DirectorCode to be upper case and A–Z only, and to be required.
   - g. Require the length to be under 400 minutes.
   - h. Require the release date to be after 1880 and before 2040.
   - i. Make the only possible choices for MovieType to be Comedy, Drama, Western, Action, or Cartoon.
   - j. Open the Directors table.
   - k. Require DirectorCode to be upper case and A–Z only, and to be required.
   - l. Open the Actors table.
   - m. Make the movienumber and actorname be required.
   - n. Use the Report Wizard to create and print a report for the Movie table.
   - o. Create a multi-table query that relates the Movie and Actors tables. Generate a query. Print the query results. Save the query.
   - p. Create a report for each table using a table Wizard. Save the reports. Print the reports.
2. Open the Races database.
   - a. Open the Daily_log table.
   - b. Delete the last two records.
   - c. Use the Report Wizard to create and print a report.
   - d. Move the comments field to the end of the table.
   - e. Open the Races table.
   - f. Make the default distance 5 and the default units "K".
   - g. Make the Date and City required fields.
   - h. Make the default state "AL" and require it to be uppercase and the letters A-Z.
   - i. Generate a report for the races table.

Internet Exercises

1. Access Information about the Crosstab Query feature of Access.
   - a. Get to the Web site for this text (http://www.prenhall.com/duffy).
   - b. Access the Web page for advanced topical coverage and then get to the above page.
   - c. You might want to print the Web page and then do the referenced hands-on exercise.
   - d. The required disk file resides with your other student files.
   - e. Print the dynaset.
2. Use the Access Assistance Library.
   - a. Access the Microsoft Web page with your browser (http://www.microsoft.com).
   - b. Click the Products button at the top of the Web page, and then choose Access 2000 for Windows from the list of products.
   - c. Click the Visit the Microsoft® Access 2000 for Windows® Website link in the Contents pane on the left side of the page.
   - d. Click the Enhancements and Assistance link.
   - e. Click the Access 2000 Assistance link.
   - f. Click the More Access Assistance link near the bottom of the page.
   - g. Browse through the links displayed on the Microsoft Access 2000 Assistance Library page. Visit any links that relate to generating reports.
   - h. Go back to the Assistance Library page.
   - i. Print the Web page.

46 Common Features of Office 2000

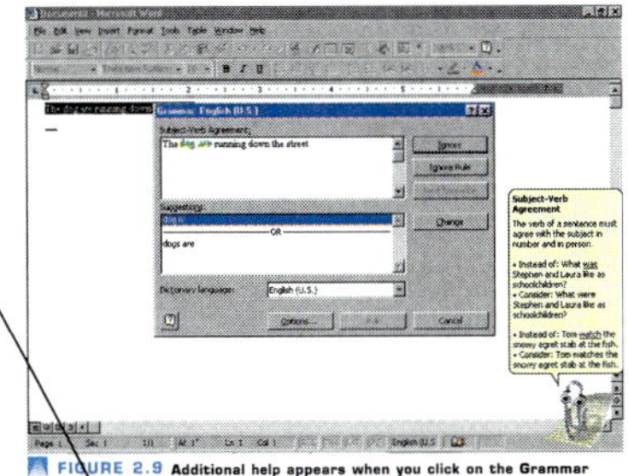

FIGURE 2.9 Additional help appears when you click on the Grammar option of the context menu.

INSERTING TEXT

Office applications default to Insert mode. **Insert mode** moves existing text in a document to the right when new characters are added. **Overwrite mode** replaces existing characters with characters that you enter from the keyboard. Press the INS key to switch from insert to overwrite mode.

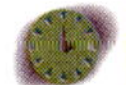

TIMELY TIP

Sometimes you will find that you are replacing text as you type. When this happens check the status line to see if the OVR indicator is on. Press the INS key to turn it off.

DELETING TEXT

You can delete text in all Office applications by first using the mouse to select the text to be deleted and then pressing DEL or BACKSPACE to delete the text. As you will see in the next part of this session, if you erroneously delete text, you can click the Undo button to restore the deleted text.

You can also delete text one character at a time. Use the DEL key to delete the character to the right of the insertion point. Use the BACKSPACE key to delete the character to the left of the insertion point.

On Your Own boxes encourage students to explore the full range of features available in Office 2000 applications.

Hands-On Exercises, based on the Running Case, give step-by-step instructions for learning each application. Numerous screen captures and button icons show students exactly what they need to know.

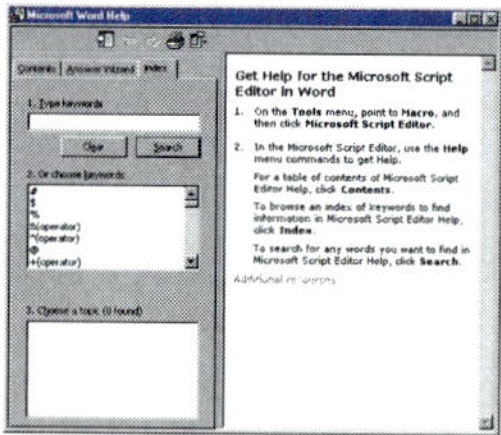

FIGURE 2.3 **The Index tab of the Word Help dialog box.**

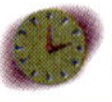

Timely Tip

You can directly access the office Help feature without going through the Office Assistant. In order to do this, you must first turn off the Office Assistant for this Word Session. This is accomplished by performing the following tasks:

1. Invoke the Office Assistant or click it to get the associated dialog box.
2. Click the options button to invoke the options dialog box.
3. Click Use the Office Assistant check box to remove the check mark. All of the checks should now dim and Office Assistant is turned off for this session.
4. The Help feature can now be invoked by pressing the F1 key or by clicking the Help button of the Standard toolbar.
5. You can later restart the Office Assistant feature by selecting the Show the Office Assistant option of the Help menu.

If you have any questions about using the Help feature, refer to Module 1: Windows 98.

On Your Own

Practice using the Help feature of Microsoft Office applications.

- Open Word and look up the following topics: Printing, Bold, Undo, Spell
- Open Excel and look up the same topics.
- If you have turned off the Office Assistant, turn it back on.

MOVING AROUND AN OFFICE DOCUMENT

Once you have opened an Office document, you are not restricted to the mouse for moving around a document. You can also use a number of common keyboard commands to position the insertion point without moving your hands from the keyboard (Table 2.1). You can issue these commands by using the keys on the ten-key number pad, or by using

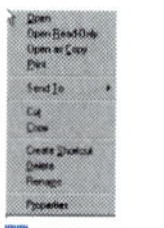

FIGURE 1.18 **The Open dialog box context menu, where you can perform many of the same file maintenance tasks that you perform in a folder window.**

Performing a Search

The Find option of the Tools menu in the Open dialog box allows you to search documents and folders. The search can be based on document names or document contents.

Performing File Maintenance

Once you have one or more documents selected in the Open dialog box, you can perform a number of tasks on them by clicking the right mouse button to open the context menu shown in Figure 1.18. For instance, you can delete, rename, print, or preview documents by using the Open dialog box context menu. These tasks are similar to ones you do on the Windows desktop or in a folder window.

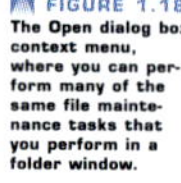

Hands-On Exercise: Opening an Existing Document

Isabel decides that she wants to examine some of the Office features that she can use to open documents. In this exercise you first examine how you can move around the disk using the Look in list box, then examine the Word document 4Ch1 Introduction to Databases. It also acquaints you with several features of the Open dialog box. You should be at the Windows desktop and should not have any applications open.

1. Open the document.

Start — Click the Start button to open the Start menu.

Programs — Click to display the Programs menu. If necessary, click the Office 2000 entry.

Microsoft Word — Click to start Word.

Open the Open dialog box by clicking this button below the menu bar. Your screen should now look like Figure 1.19. You should see any documents that occupy the My Documents folder on the disk (yours will look differently than Figure 1.19). This is the default folder displayed by Microsoft Office whenever an Open command is issued.

Look in — Click this entry of the Look in list box to display a list of available storage resources (Figure 1.20).

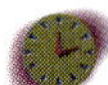

Timely Tip

You may try to open a file at some time and receive a dialog box with a Browse button. When the Browse button is clicked, a dialog box very similar to an Open dialog box appears allowing you to move through directories or switch disks to locate a desired file.

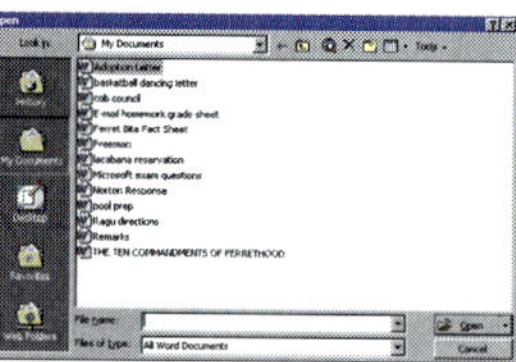

FIGURE 1.19 **The Open dialog box with the documents that reside in the My Documents folder (the Office default storage area). Yours will look different.**

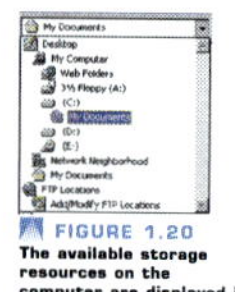

FIGURE 1.20 **The available storage resources on the computer are displayed in the Look in list box.**

2. If necessary, activate the area containing your student files. This example assumes that those student files reside on drive A. If your files reside on a network drive or in a directory on a fixed disk, your instructor will provide you with the proper command sequence. Be sure to write down that command sequence so you can use it in the future.

3½ Floppy (A:) — Click the drive A option to display a list of documents that reside on that drive (Figure 1.21). If the Open dialog box does not list the documents as shown in Figure 1.21, click the List option of the View pull-down menu.

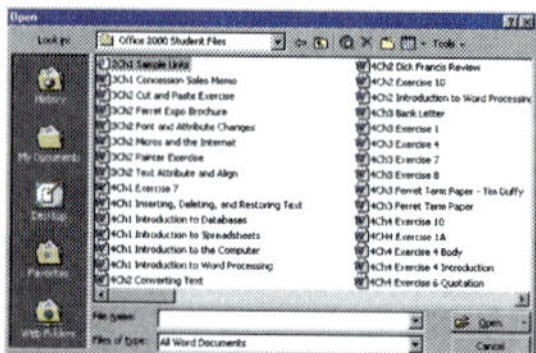

FIGURE 1.21 **The documents that accompany the textbook (your display may be different).**

3. Open a document by double-clicking a document name.

4Ch1 Introduction to Databases Double-click this file name. Microsoft Word loads the document. You should now see a screen like that shown in Figure 1.22.

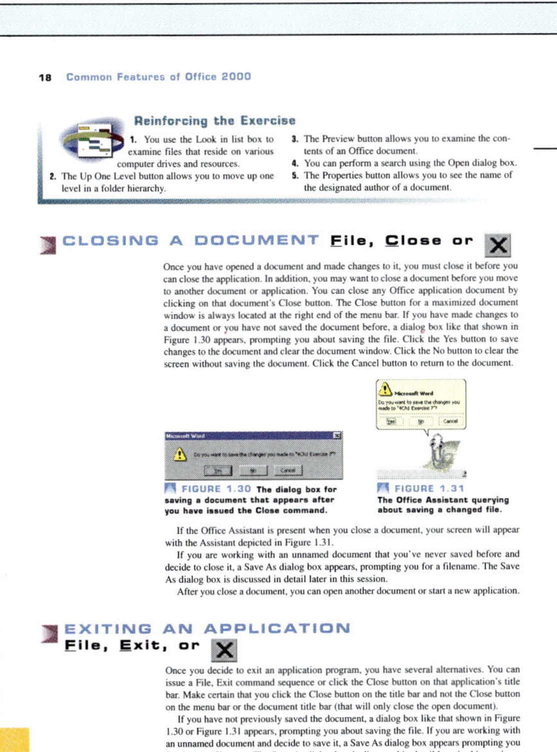

18 Common Features of Office 2000

Reinforcing the Exercise

1. You use the Look in list box to examine files that reside on various computer drives and resources.
2. The Up One Level button allows you to move up one level in a folder hierarchy.
3. The Preview button allows you to examine the contents of an Office document.
4. You can perform a search using the Open dialog box.
5. The Properties button allows you to see the name of the designated author of a document.

CLOSING A DOCUMENT File, Close or X

Once you have opened a document and made changes to it, you must close it before you can close the application. In addition, you may want to close a document before you move to another document or application. You can close any Office application document by clicking on that document's Close button. The Close button for a maximized document window is always located at the right end of the menu bar. If you have made changes to a document or you have not saved the document before, a dialog box like that shown in Figure 1.30 appears, prompting you about saving the file. Click the Yes button to save changes to the document and clear the document window. Click the No button to clear the screen without saving the document. Click the Cancel button to return to the document.

FIGURE 1.30 The dialog box for saving a document that appears after you have issued the Close command.

FIGURE 1.31 The Office Assistant querying about saving a changed file.

If the Office Assistant is present when you close a document, your screen will appear with the Assistant depicted in Figure 1.31.

If you are working with an unnamed document that you've never saved before and decide to close it, a Save As dialog box appears, prompting you for a filename. The Save As dialog box is discussed in detail later in this session.

After you close a document, you can open another document or start a new application.

EXITING AN APPLICATION File, Exit, or X

Once you decide to exit an application program, you have several alternatives. You can issue a File, Exit command sequence or click the Close button on that application's title bar. Make certain that you click the Close button on the title bar and not the Close button on the menu bar or the document title bar (that will only close the open document).

If you have not previously saved the document, a dialog box like that shown in Figure 1.30 or Figure 1.31 appears, prompting you about saving the file. If you are working with an unnamed document and decide to save it, a Save As dialog box appears prompting you for the new filename. The Save As dialog box is discussed in detail later in this session.

Reinforcing the Exercise sections help students recall and refer to the work they have completed.

Tables of keyboard or **toolbar icons and symbols** provide students with quick reference to the conventions and uses of Office 2000 applications.

Using Common Document-Related Commands 29

MANIPULATING THE PREVIEWED DOCUMENT

A number of buttons appear at the top of the Preview window that you can use to manipulate the previewed document. These buttons are summarized in Table 1.5. The menu bar also appears in the Preview window, so you can issue commands from it to change the appearance of the previewed document. You can also make any changes to the text of the document that are required while in Print Preview mode.

TABLE 1.5 Preview Window Buttons

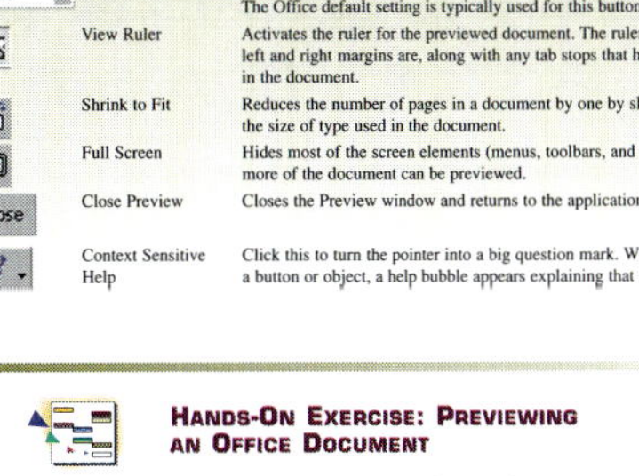

Button	Name of Button	Function
	Print	Sends the document immediately to the printer. No Print dialog box is displayed.
	Magnifier	Changes the pointer to a magnifying glass. Click the part of the document you want magnified. Click that part again to return it to its original size.
	One Page	Displays one page of the document at a time.
	Multiple Pages	Displays a menu that allows you to determine the number of pages to be displayed at one time.
19%	Zoom	Controls the size of the simulated text displayed in the Preview window. The Office default setting is typically used for this button.
	View Ruler	Activates the ruler for the previewed document. The ruler shows where the left and right margins are, along with any tab stops that have been included in the document.
	Shrink to Fit	Reduces the number of pages in a document by one by slightly changing the size of type used in the document.
	Full Screen	Hides most of the screen elements (menus, toolbars, and so forth) so that more of the document can be previewed.
Close	Close Preview	Closes the Preview window and returns to the application window.
	Context Sensitive Help	Click this to turn the pointer into a big question mark. When you now click a button or object, a help bubble appears explaining that item.

HANDS-ON EXERCISE: PREVIEWING AN OFFICE DOCUMENT

Isabel wants to use the Print Preview feature to demonstrate to several of the secretaries how easy it is to see exactly how a file will print. She also wants to demonstrate the effects of several of the Preview window buttons.

This exercise examines the Print Preview feature by using the Word document 4Ch1 Introduction to Word Processing. It assumes that you have Word started.

1. Open the document.

Open the Open dialog box by clicking this toolbar button. If necessary, select the drive and/or folder in the Look in list that contains your student files.

COMPANION WEB SITE

The Companion Web Site is an on-line learning environment for instructors and students. The range of activities available in Companion Web Sites includes:

- *On-line Study Guide*—different types of self-assessment exercises including multiple choice, true/false, and fill-in-the-blank questions, with instant feedback available at the click of button.
- *Internet Exercises*—take the text feature one step further by providing the links in the exercises. The Companion Web Site extends the exercises by providing an interactive experience for students as they complete exercises in the text that send them to the site for information or files. The textbook uses this feature to introduce a number of advanced software topics and provides the same type of topical coverage, Hands-On Exercises, and Reinforcing the Exercise found in the regular textbook.
- *Password Protected Faculty Resources*—ancillary materials accessible for instant download, syllabus creation, and management tools are integrated into the Companion Web Site, including PowerPoint slides written by Tim Duffy, as well as a text art library.
- *Student Data Files*—The student data files required for hands-on exercises and end of session exercises can be downloaded from this location.
- *Syllabus Manager*—an online syllabus creation and management utility. Syllabus Manager™ provides instructors with an easy, step-by-step process to create and revise syllabi, with direct links into Companion Web Site and other online content. Students access Syllabus Manager™ directly from within the Companion Web Site, providing quick access to course assignments.

TEST MANAGER

Test Manager™ is a comprehensive suite of tools for testing and assessment. Test Manager™ allows educators to easily create and distribute tests for their courses, either by printing and distributing through traditional methods or by on-line delivery via a Local Area Network (LAN) server. Four question formats are available: multiple choice, true/false, matching, and completion exercises. Answer keys and page references for test questions are provided.

PRINTED INSTRUCTOR'S MANUAL BY BILL DALEY AND TIM DUFFY

The printed Instructor's Manual includes a Test Bank and Transparency Masters for each project in the student text. The Test Bank contains tests with answers and consists of multiple choice, true/false, and fill-in questions that refer to pages in the student text. Transparency Masters illustrate key concepts and screen captures from the text. The Instructor's Manual also offers teaching notes to help integrate current technology (such as the text Web site) into a modern course on Office 2000; objectives and outline for each session; and grading tips.

INSTRUCTOR'S CD-ROM

Instructors get extra support for this text from supplemental materials. The Instructor's Resource CD-ROM contains screen captures, diagrams and tables from the text, as well as files that correspond to key figures in the book. These can be incorporated into PowerPoint electronic slides that professors can create for their classes. Screen-by-screen steps in a project can be displayed in class or reviewed by students in the computer lab. The Instructor's Resource CD-ROM includes the entire Instructor's Manual with Test Bank in Microsoft Word. It also includes text-based PowerPoint presentation slides that support classroom lectures for each session. Six slides can be printed per page and distributed to students to facilitate notetaking. A Computerized Test Bank is included to create printed tests or network tests. Student data files and completed data files are also on the Instructor's Resource CD-ROM. All the electronic files can be found on the instructor's password protected Web site at http://www.prenhall.com/duffy. Contact your Sales Representative for your ID and password.

STUDENT SUPPLEMENTS

SKILLCHECK Assessment Software is a network-based skills assessment-testing program available through the Prentice Hall Point Program. SKILLCHECK measures student proficiency with Word 2000, Excel 2000, Access 2000, and PowerPoint 2000. Through a completely customizable set of test options or by using the pre-loaded MOUS certification review exams, professors select the tasks to be tested and receive student results immediately. The test is taken in a simulated software environment, which enables the software to run on network or individual computers. On-screen instructions require students to perform tasks as though they were using the actual application. The program automatically records responses, assesses student accuracy, and reports the resulting score in a printout or disk file as well as to the instructor's grade book. Results can also be downloaded as an Excel file.

COURSE KITS

The Duffy Office 2000 applications texts are available separately or in a single *Microsoft® Office 2000 Professional* volume. The Office 2000 Professional suite includes Common Features of Office 2000, Windows® 98, Internet Explorer 5, Word 2000, Access 2000, Excel 2000, PowerPoint 2000, Outlook® 2000, and FrontPage® 2000. Available as a separate module is Web Collaboration Tools, which includes Outlook® 2000, FrontPage® 2000, and Internet Explorer 5. Whether you package the entire Office 2000 suite with our concepts books or the individual modules, your students will receive a significant discount.

PRENTICE HALL POINTS PROGRAM

As a publisher, we are aware of the need to have the most current software application programs available to students in introductory computer courses. We are pleased to partner with colleges and universities to achieve this goal through our Prentice Hall Points Program.

By adopting our text and lab books, your school may qualify for free software programs and site licenses to be used by your students in your school's computer lab.

ACKNOWLEDGMENTS

I am amazed that seventeen years have passed since I started the first edition of Four Software Tools. At that time, I was completely unaware of the time-consuming efforts needed to produce a college-level textbook. Since then, however, I have developed a sincere appreciation of what is required to make a successful text. The success formula includes family, friends, colleagues, and many individuals in the publishing business. I remain deeply indebted to my wife, Wendy, who encouraged me to write the original version of Four Software Tools. Without her encouragement, the original text never would have been finished, and without her continued support, these projects would be impossible to accomplish.

Keith Hallmark at Calhoun Community College helped draft the interdisciplinary exercises, and Bill Daley from the University of Oregon wrote the Companion Web Site student study guide questions—many thanks for a job well done. I also want to express my sincere appreciation to the reviewers of this manuscript:

Michael Barrett, *Clarion University*
Jill Betts, *Tyler Junior College*
Bill Daley, *University of Oregon*
Kathryn A. Drexel, *Drexel Associates*
Peter Drexel, *Plymouth State College*
Keith Hallmark, *Calhoun Community College*
Albert L. Harris, *Appalachian State University*
Seth Hock, *Columbus State Community College*
Cynthia Johnson, *University of Central Florida*
Marie McCooey, *Bryant College*
Randall J. Molmen, *Baldwin–Wallace College*
Vincent J. Motto, *Asnuntuck Community–Technical College*
Stephen C. Solosky, *Nassau Community College*
Donald M. Stasiw, *Utica College of Syracuse University*
Barbara Z. Taylor, *Elon College*
Melinda C. White, *Santa Fe Community College*
Bob Williams, *Clinton Community College*
Dr. Andrew Yang, *Southern Connecticut State*

Individuals at the publishing company also play an important role. Addison Wesley Longman's editorial staff is superb. With warm feelings, I would like to acknowledge Anita Devine and Ed Moura. Maureen Allaire initially signed this book, and over the years she has had much to do with many of my books. I am pleased to have worked with Anita Devine, who brings a wealth of editorial experience in microcomputer texts. Ed Moura, Editor-in-Chief, brought a number of excellent ideas to this project. Holly Rioux, Assistant Editor, made certain that everything was moving on an even keel. Deanna Storey's attention to detail and the review process helped shape this project and make this edition happen. Martha Johnson, Emily Kim, and Ann Sargent's copyedits and technical edits helped to assure internal consistency of the text. This is the first time I have worked with Michele Heinz and Elm Street Publishing Services—they have been wonderful to work with.

A dedication is not complete without including my son, Michael. Michael continues to make any writing project a challenge. His requests to go biking, golfing, swimming, or pursuing a new interest are much appreciated. Michael especially likes to surf the Web to complete homework assignments and has become a twelve-year-old master at ferreting out information from the Web.

Microsoft® Windows® 98

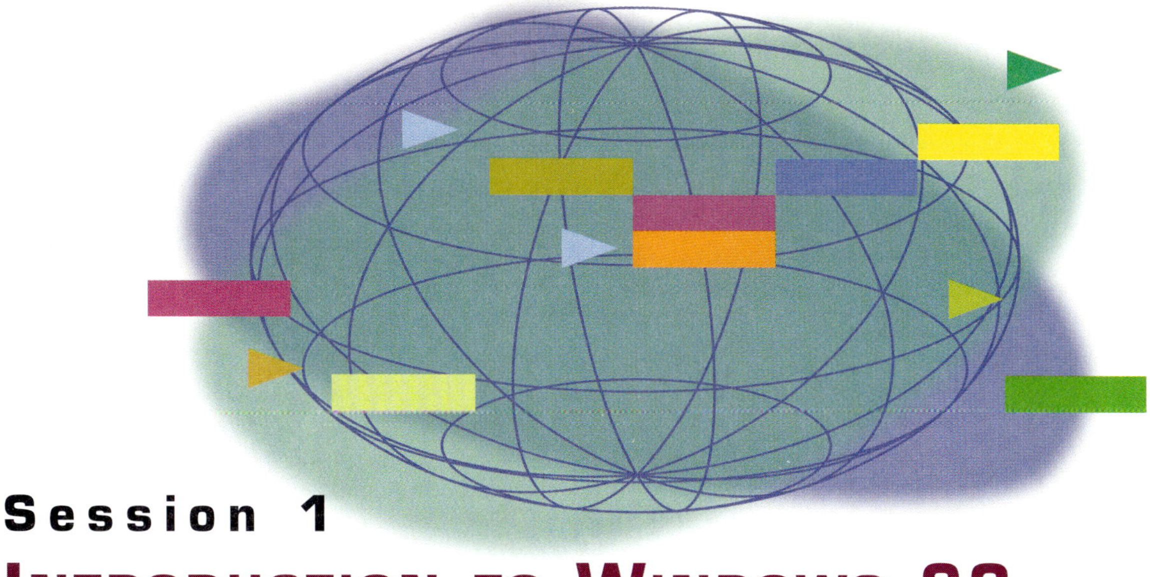

Session 1
Introduction to Windows 98

After completing this session, you should be able to:

- Define a graphic user interface (GUI)
- Start the computer system and Windows
- Exit Windows and turn off the computer
- Control the desktop appearance
- Identify and use various components of the Windows desktop
- Identify and use components of a window
- Identify and use the taskbar
- Use dialog boxes

Windows 95 was the first true combination of operating system and graphical user interface for Intel-based computers. It made it easier for you to use your computer and the software that resided on that computer. Windows 98 is a logical extension of Windows 95. It builds on many of the features that were introduced in the prior version and operates the computer more efficiently. In addition, it integrates World Wide Web (WWW) capabilities into the way you use the operating system. Many features of the WWW are always at your grasp.

An **operating system** is a complex set of computer instructions that lies between you, the person using the computer, and the computer itself. It accepts a command from the user, evaluates that command, and then executes the command. It is the operating system that makes a computer usable for human beings.

A **graphical user interface (GUI)** is a software program that allows you to communicate with your computer by using a pointing device called a **mouse**. In most instances, a mouse allows you to perform a task more quickly than a text-based environment, in which you perform tasks by entering many keystrokes from the keyboard.

Prior to the introduction of Windows 95, you had to first start the computer, which then loaded the disk operating system. A **disk operating system (DOS)** is a set of programs that allows the user to interact with the computer. After the operating system started, the older Windows program began. In this type of environment, you had to know how to use both DOS and Windows.

THE WINDOWS 98 ENVIRONMENT

Windows 95, introduced in August 1995, folded DOS into a new GUI. This meant that you only needed to know how to use the Windows graphic user interface. In addition, the easy-to-understand version of the Windows GUI allowed a beginner to get started quickly using a computer and learning how to use and interact with application software.

Windows 98 was introduced in June 1998. It continues to expand and enhance the features that were introduced in the 95 version of the operating system and also greatly enhances the ability of Windows to interact with the World Wide Web. As you will see, the way Windows appears to the everyday user is quite similar to the way many people use to browse pages on the Web.

STARTING WINDOWS

To start Windows 98, you just start your computer. Once you turn on the computer, Windows 98 loads automatically. During this startup process, you may see a screen that looks like a Microsoft flag. When Windows has completely loaded you will see a screen called the desktop.

THE WINDOWS DESKTOP

Once Windows has finished loading, the desktop appears on your screen. The **desktop** (Figure 1.1) is a workspace (much like the top of a desk) on which you can find a great number of your Windows tools and perform a variety of tasks. Images appearing here might allow you to start a program, open a document stored on your system, or even connect to a Web site.

This desktop provides a work area for each session that you have with Windows. When you start an application, it will appear as a window on the desktop. The desktop shown in Figure 1.1 may differ from the one currently on your screen. You may see a different background color, different items displayed, and have the ability to interact differently with your desktop. You can customize Windows in just about any way you want. The differences between the appearance of the desktops will be discussed shortly.

TIMELY TIP

Many computers in a classroom environment are hooked to local area networks and require that each student log onto the system using a special user name or identification (ID) and password. If you are operating in such an environment, your instructor will provide you with a logon ID. You will determine your password. Do not tell anyone your password, because anyone who knows your password can log onto the system with your name.

In this type of environment, after Windows starts, a box appears requesting your user name and password. Enter your user name. Press TAB to move the cursor to the Password text box, and enter your password. The letters that you type do not appear in the box (they are replaced by asterisks), because you don't want any other people to see your password.

After you have finished entering this information, Windows finishes loading.

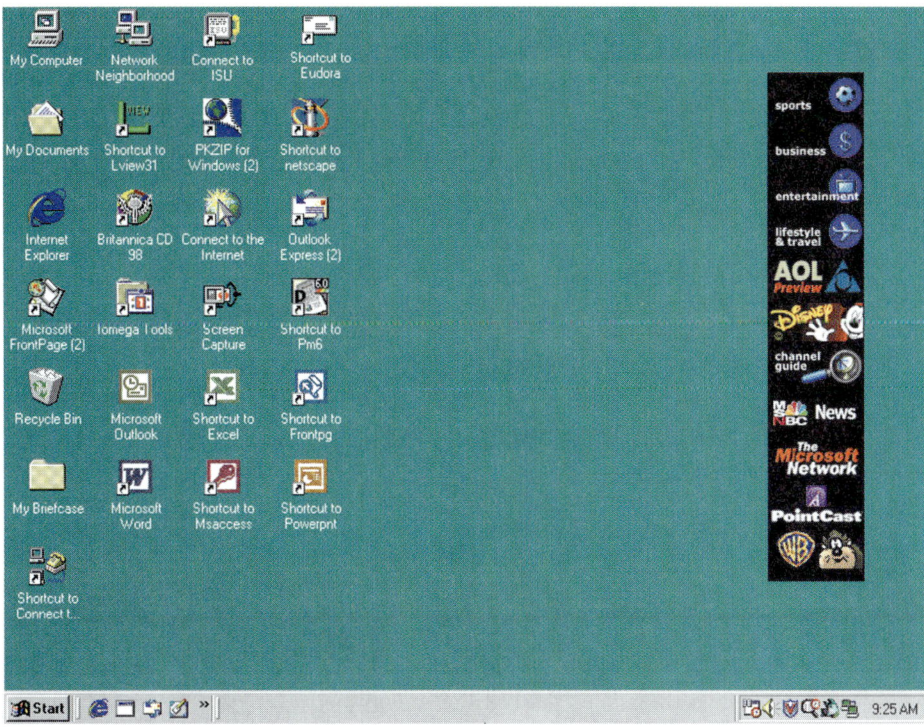

FIGURE 1.1 The Windows desktop.

Desktop Objects

Any image or item that appears on the desktop is called an **object**. As we progress through the various modules in this text, you will see many different types of objects, including documents, fields in a database, and buttons on a toolbar. A graphic representation of an object is called an **icon**. Common icons on the desktop include My Computer, Outlook Express, Recycle Bin, and My Documents.

An object always has **properties**. Properties control how an object behaves and operates in a Windows environment. You control the properties of an object via a properties sheet. (You will learn more about properties when you use the applications in later modules.) The background color of the Windows desktop is an example of a property. For now, remember that all Windows applications make use of the concepts of objects, and all objects have properties.

EXAMINING THE WINDOWS DESKTOP

In the Windows 98 environment, you make extensive use of the mouse as a pointing device and as a method of entering many different commands. While this environment does allow you to use the keyboard, it is usually considered to be more cumbersome compared to the mouse for beginning users of Windows. Nevertheless, some of the more frequently used keyboard commands called **keyboard shortcuts** will be introduced from time to time.

The mouse pointer is a large white arrow that appears on-screen. This image moves as you move the mouse on your workspace. You can use a mouse to take the actions listed in Table 1.1.

TABLE 1.1 Mouse Actions

Point	Move the mouse so that the pointer rests on a part of the screen (an icon or command, for instance).
Click	Quickly press and release the left mouse button. If an object is underlined (Web characteristics have been assigned to it), clicking an object once will start an application or open a window. If there is no underline, clicking an object once will merely select it. To deselect something, click any unused area of the desktop.
Right-click	Use the right button to invoke a **context menu**, as shown in Figure 1.3. This menu shows the most frequently used commands for that object. To get rid of the context menu, click any unused area of the desktop.
Double-click	Press and release the left mouse button twice rapidly in succession. You often use this operation to start an application represented by an icon (Web characteristics have not been applied).
Drag	Press and hold the left mouse button while moving the mouse. Use this operation to include multiple lines or cells in a selected block to be operated on by a subsequent command. It can also be used to move an object to another location. When you have reached the ending location, release the mouse button.
Deselect	Click anywhere on a blank area of the screen.

TIMELY TIP

A computer mouse can have many different characteristics. It may, for example, have three mouse buttons. If that is the case, the middle button is programmable, or user-definable. This book makes use of only the left and right mouse buttons, regardless of whether you use a two- or three-button mouse.

You can also substitute a trackball for a mouse. A trackball is similar to a mouse except that it appears to be upside down, with the ball on the top. The advantage of a trackball is that you do not need an area of your workspace cleared to move the mouse around. A trackball can also have either two or three buttons.

Unless you have set up (or configured) Windows differently, you will use the left mouse button to issue any instructions. Some people configure Windows to switch the buttons and, therefore, use the opposite button than the one indicated.

When you are using the mouse, the shape of the pointer provides valuable information. For instance, the shape of the pointer tells you when you are performing a normal selection, selecting text, resizing a window, or moving a window. Various possible shapes of the pointer are shown in Table 1.2.

TABLE 1.2 Pointer Shapes and Their Meanings

	Normal Select		Text Select		Horizontal Resize
	Help Select		Handwriting		Diagonal Resize 1
	Working in Background		Link Select		Diagonal Resize 2
	Busy		Unavailable		Move
	Precision Select		Vertical Resize		Alternate Select

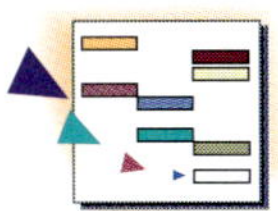

Hands-On Exercise: Using the Mouse

1. Practice moving the mouse. Get a feel for how your hand movement affects the movement of the pointer. As you perform the following exercises, notice how the pointer moves on-screen.

Move the mouse away from you.

Move the mouse toward you.

Move the mouse to the right.

Move the mouse to the left.

Move the mouse diagonally.

Practice moving the pointer on the screen until you feel comfortable using the mouse.

2. Select an object (no underline appears).

Position the pointer on the My Computer icon on the desktop.

Click Click the left mouse button to select the My Computer object. The icon should now appear blue, indicating that it has been selected. Note the position of this icon. If the object was underlined, a separate window appears like that depicted in Figure 1.7. Use Step 9 instructions to close the window.

Drag Click and drag the My Computer icon to the lower-right corner of the desktop (Figure 1.2).

Drag Drag the My Computer icon back to its original location at the top of the screen.

Timely Tip

If your My Computer icon does not move as it should, you may have to reset how Windows arranges icons on the desktop. This is accomplished by right-clicking the mouse on an unused area of the desktop to invoke the context menu. Select the Arrange Icons option and then select the by Auto Arrange option. You should now be able to move the My Computer icon.

FIGURE 1.2 **The My Computer icon in a new location on the desktop.**

3. Deselect the My Computer icon.

Click Click anywhere in the blank area of the desktop to deselect the icon.

4. Open a context menu.

Right-click Place the pointer in an unused area of the desktop and click the right mouse button. A context menu appears (Figure 1.3).

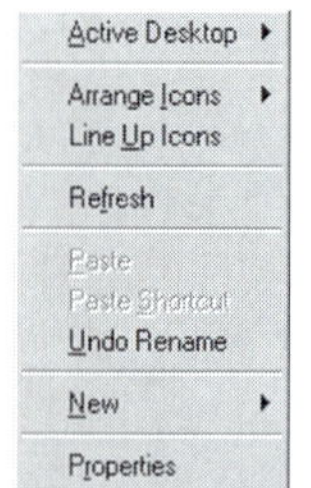

FIGURE 1.3 **The context menu for the desktop.**

5. Close the context menu.

Click Place the pointer in an unused area of the desktop and click the left mouse button.

6. Open the context menu for the My Computer object.

Right-click Place the pointer on the My Computer icon and click the right mouse button. The context menu appears as shown in Figure 1.4. Notice that the contents of the two context menus differ. The options that appear on the context menu depend on the object that you right-clicked.

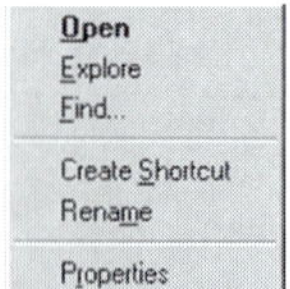

FIGURE 1.4 **The context menu for the My Computer object.**

7. Close the context menu.

Click Place the pointer in an unused area of the desktop and click the left mouse button.

8. Open the My Computer window by double-clicking (if underlined, single-click).

Double-click Position the pointer on the My Computer icon and double-click the left mouse button. The window shown in Figure 1.5 appears (your window may look different). The appearance and function of a window are discussed in more detail later in this session.

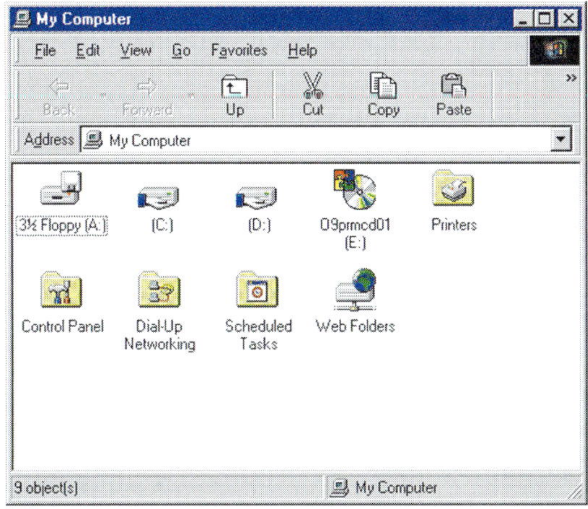

FIGURE 1.5 The My Computer window.

9. Close the My Computer window.

Click the Close button in the upper-right corner of the My Computer window to close it.

Reinforcing the Exercise

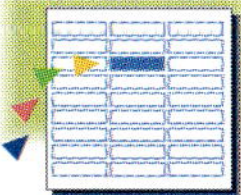

1. A context menu opens when you right-click an object.
2. To perform a drag-and-drop operation, you click an object and continue holding down the left mouse button as you move the pointer. You let go of the mouse button when you want to release the object.
3. Close a context menu by clicking any unused area of the desktop.
4. You open an object or application represented by an icon by double-clicking that icon.
5. Close a window by clicking on the Close button.

On Your Own

After you have gotten acquainted with Windows, you might decide that you want to change the characteristics of your mouse. This requires using the command sequence Start, Settings, Control Panel to activate the Control Panel window. Double-click the Mouse icon to invoke the Mouse Properties dialog box. Make any changes that you think are appropriate. DO NOT DO THIS until you feel comfortable with Windows.

Using ToolTips

Windows 98 makes use of a feature referred to as a **ToolTip** to provide you with information about an icon, feature, or part of a window that appears on the desktop.

Hands-On Exercise: Using ToolTips

1. Start from the desktop with all windows closed.

2. Position the mouse pointer to the My Computer icon and keep it there until the ToolTip shown in Figure 1.6 appears.

3. If it is present, position the mouse pointer to the Internet Explorer Channel Bar and keep it there until the ToolTip shown in Figure 1.7 appears.

FIGURE 1.6 The ToolTip for the My Computer icon.

FIGURE 1.7 The ToolTip for the Warner Bros button of the Internet Explorer Channel Bar.

4. Point to the Start button until the ToolTip appears.

5. Point to the time in the lower right-hand corner of the screen to get a ToolTip.

6. Open the My Computer window and position the mouse over the Close  **button of the window.** A ToolTip appears.

7. Close the My Computer window.

Reinforcing the Exercise

1. A ToolTip contains explanatory text about an object that appears on the desktop.
2. A ToolTip appears when the mouse is positioned over an object.
3. A ToolTip can be used to identify a button in a window.

Examining Some Desktop Objects

The following sections summarize some objects typically found on the Windows desktop.

My Computer

The **My Computer** icon opens a window that displays information about the resources of your computer, such as printers, the disk drive(s), fixed disk(s), and the CD-ROM drive, if any. By double-clicking on the icon that represents one of these storage devices, you can see what folders and files that device contains.

It also allows you to access system configuration data as well as any modem links to an Internet provider (if any have been installed on your computer).

Outlook Express

The **Outlook Express** icon allows you to access Microsoft's E-mail software, Outlook Express. You use this software to send and receive E-mail messages as well as faxes over a network or via an Internet provider. Your instructor will provide access information for Outlook Express, if it has been installed at your site.

Recycle Bin

The **Recycle Bin** provides a repository for deleted documents. With the Recycle Bin, you can easily restore documents you have inadvertently erased.

Internet Explorer Channel Bar

If it is present on your desktop, the **Internet Explorer Channel Bar** provides access to a number of Web sites via your Web browser (discussed in Module 2). Any channels that you have subscribed to appear on the Channel Bar. To view the content of a channel, click the appropriate button. Figure 1.8 shows the Warner Bros. channel Web page accessed and shown via the Internet Explorer browser software.

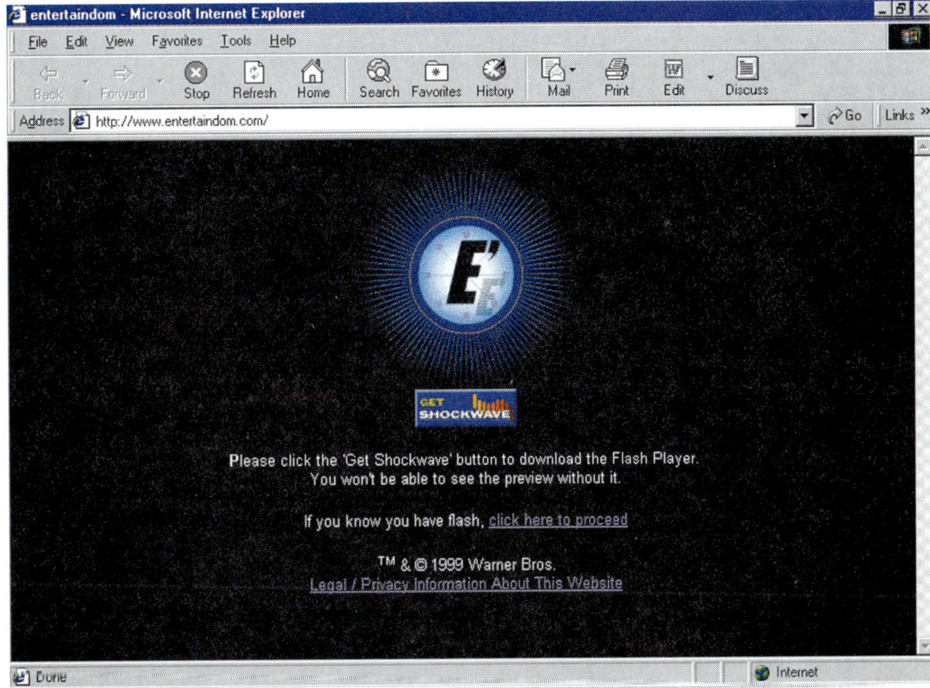

FIGURE 1.8 The Warner Bros. Channel Web page displayed using Internet Explorer.

Taskbar

The **taskbar** is the gray bar that usually appears at the bottom of the desktop. As you will see later in this session, you can quickly shift from one application to another by clicking the application buttons displayed in the taskbar. The application buttons represent open windows or programs that have been started and are currently running in windows.

The **status area** (also called the **system tray**) at the far right end of the taskbar displays miniature icons representing small programs that are always in memory (like the clock).

The Start button appears at the far left end of the taskbar and is discussed separately below.

The taskbar may also have one or more toolbars present. A **toolbar** contains buttons that, when clicked, can launch a program or execute a command instead of going through a menu structure. Figure 1.1 shows the Quick Launch toolbar that can be used to easily start (launch) several Microsoft programs like Internet Explorer, Outlook Express, close all windows and display only the desktop, or launch Internet Explorer with the Channel Bar present.

The taskbar does not always have to appear at the bottom of the screen. Using a drag operation, it can be moved to any side of the desktop or even enlarged.

START BUTTON

The **Start button** is located at the left end of the taskbar. It provides a click's access to programs, documents, settings, and other types of objects (Figure 1.9). It also provides the only safe way to exit Windows. Some menu choices contain a right-hand arrow indicating that additional choices are available on an additional menu that appears when you place your pointer over such a menu option. Figure 1.9 shows the menus that can be displayed via the Start, Programs, Accessories, Games menu sequence. Table 1.3 discusses the various menu options that are displayed in the Start menu.

If a menu is too long to display at one time, positioning arrows appear at the top and bottom of the menu. Such a positioning button can be found at the bottom of the Programs menu. This indicates that more options than those that appear are contained in the menu. To see more options position the mouse on the appropriate arrow until the desired option appears.

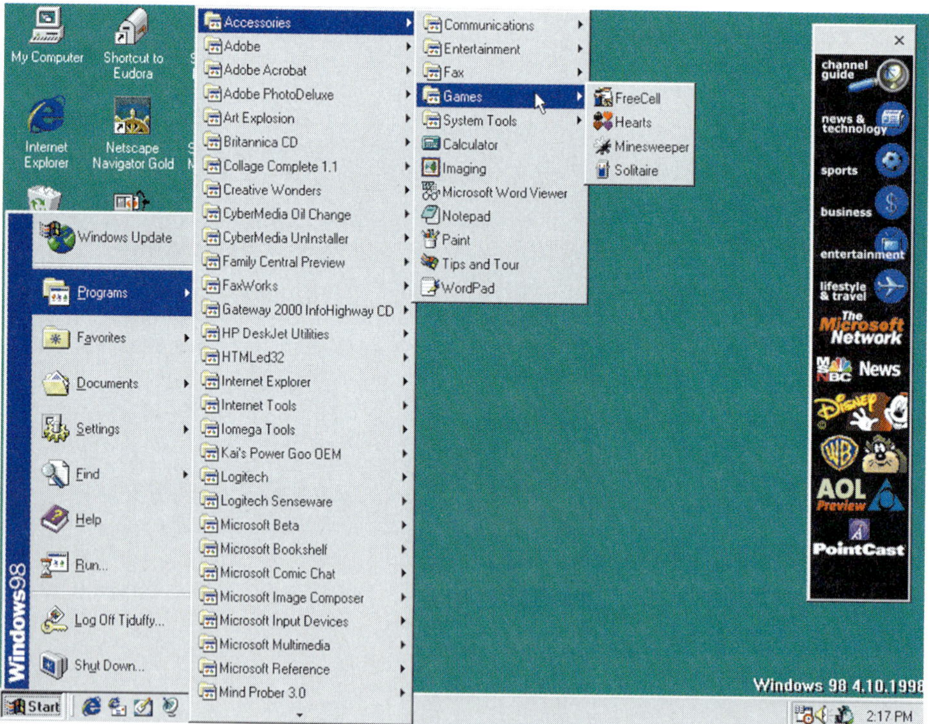

FIGURE 1.9 The Accessories menu accessed via the Start, Programs, Accessories, Games menu sequence.

TABLE 1.3 Options of the Start Menu

Windows Update	Get updates for Windows directly from the Microsoft Web site.
Programs	View a list of programs that have been installed for your computer.
Favorites	Open your favorite files or Web Pages.
Documents	Open a recently used document.
Settings	Modify system settings using the Control Panel, select or install printers, change the taskbar or Start menu, and so forth.
Find	Search for files, folders, search the Internet, or try to use a "people finder" service on the Internet.
Help	Get answers to any questions that you have about Windows 98.
Run	Open items such as Web pages, programs, and other computers' resources.
Log Off	Log off a Windows session so that the computer can be used by another person.
Shut Down	Shut down or restart your computer.

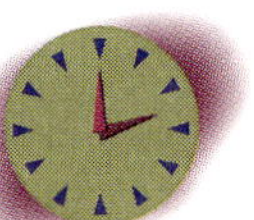

TIMELY TIP

Some computer keyboards come equipped with a windows key that, when pressed, automatically displays the Start menu. You may want to check your keyboard to see if there are any keys with the Windows flag on it. If there is, see if pressing it makes the Start menu appear.

OPENING MULTIPLE WINDOWS

Clicking or double-clicking an object on the desktop often causes a window to open. If one window already appears on-screen and you open another, the second window overlaps the first. This means that you may, at any time, have multiple windows visible on-screen. The window that appears on top is called the **active window**. Other windows beneath the active window are called **inactive windows**. When you click anywhere on an inactive window, it becomes the active window and has a colored rather than gray title bar.

When you have multiple application windows open at one time, Windows is running each of these programs simultaneously. This Windows capability is called **multitasking**.

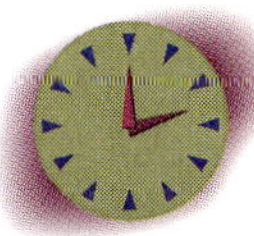

TIMELY TIP

When several buttons appear on the taskbar, you can click a button to move from one window or application to another.

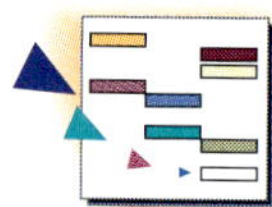

Hands-On Exercise: Examining Windows Objects

1. Open the My Computer window.

Double-click Double-click the My Computer icon. The My Computer window appears (Figure 1.10).

2. Open the window for drive C.

(C:)

Double-click the drive C icon. (Your drive C icon may be labeled differently from that shown in Figure 1.10.) The window shown in Figure 1.11 appears, showing the contents of drive C. The folder icons represent other storage areas, while the other icons represent specific files of data. Notice that the two windows displayed overlap one another, and the drive C window is currently the active window.

Timely Tip

The following settings have been used for the subsequent figures in this textbook.

The display of multiple windows is controlled by issuing the command sequence from the My Computer window: View, Folder Options to invoke the Folders Options dialog box; then click the Classic style option of the General tab.

To get the small icons, issue the View, List command sequence.

3. Make the My Computer window the active window.

Click Click any part of the My Computer window. (If two windows do not appear on your screen, click the My Computer button on the taskbar.) Your desktop should now appear as shown in Figure 1.12. Notice also that Windows has placed two buttons on the taskbar: one for the My Computer open window and the other for the drive C window. The icon for the active window appears highlighted or pressed in.

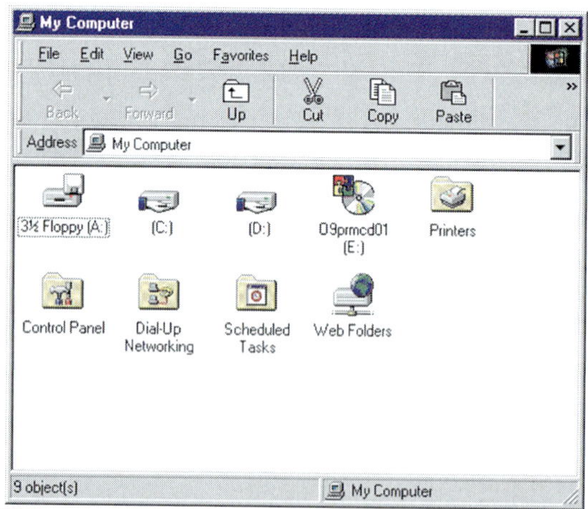

FIGURE 1.10 The My Computer window.

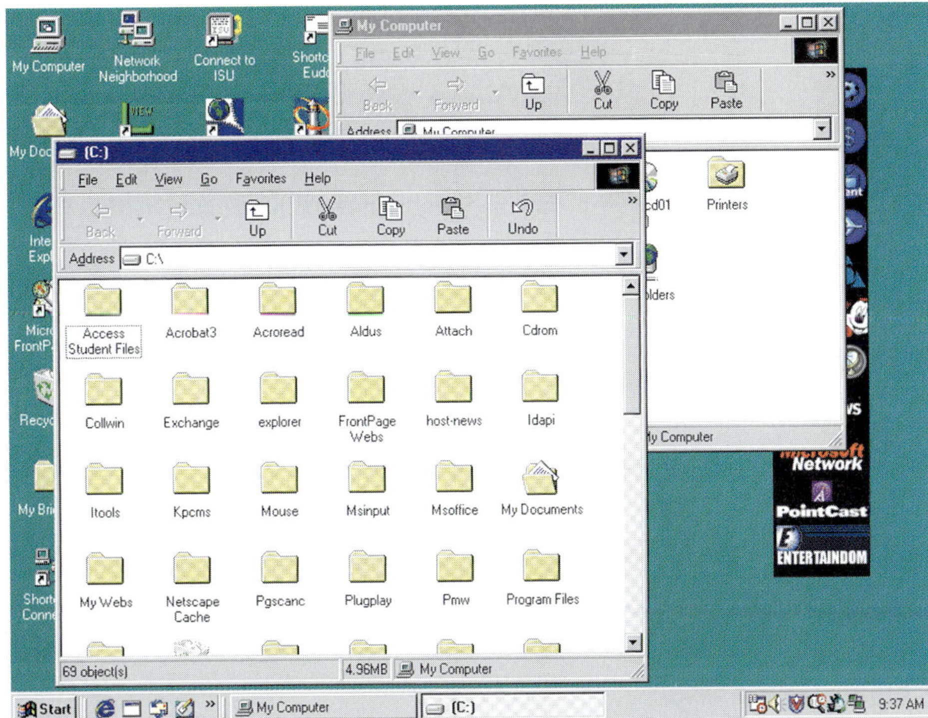

FIGURE 1.11 **The window showing the contents of drive C. Note the buttons on the taskbar.**

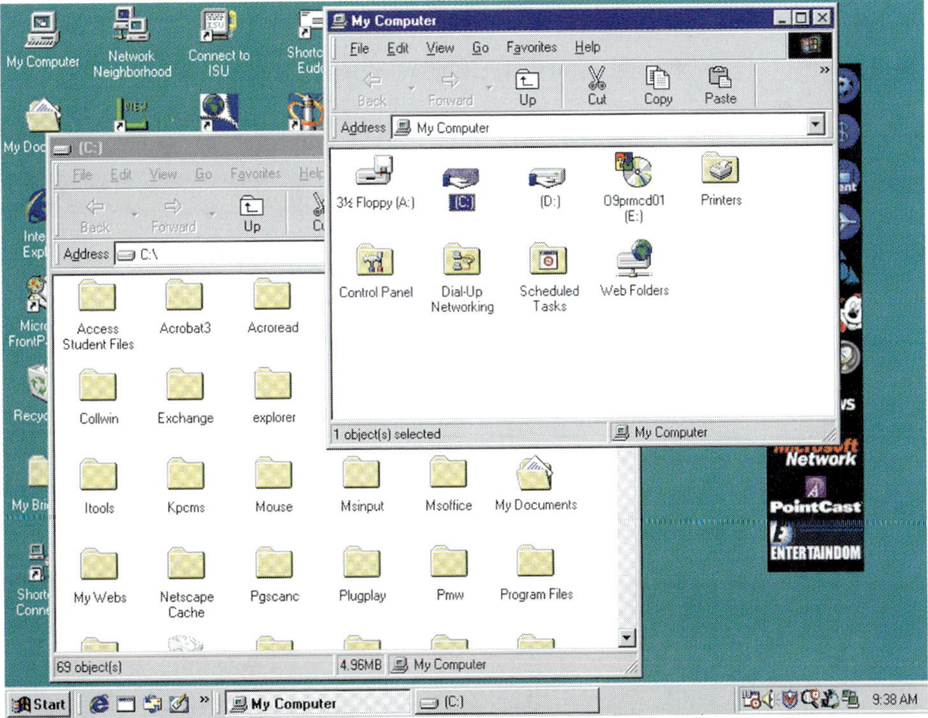

FIGURE 1.12 **The Windows desktop with the active My Computer window on top of the drive C window.**

4. Close the two open windows.

Click the Close button at the top of the My Computer window. The My Computer window should now disappear.

Click the Close button at the top of the drive C window. The drive C window should now disappear.

5. Examine any files that have been deleted recently.

Position the pointer on the Recycle Bin icon and double-click the left mouse button. A window like that shown in Figure 1.13 should appear (you should see different file names). To restore a deleted file requires that you right-click the mouse on the desired file and then select Restore from the context menu.

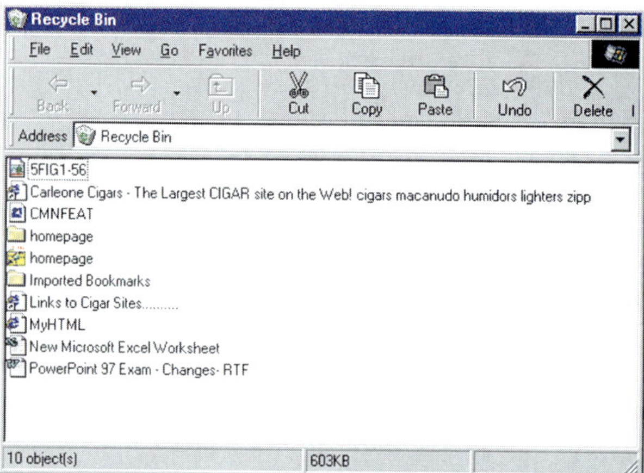

FIGURE 1.13 The Recycle Bin allows you to restore data that has been inadvertently deleted from your computer.

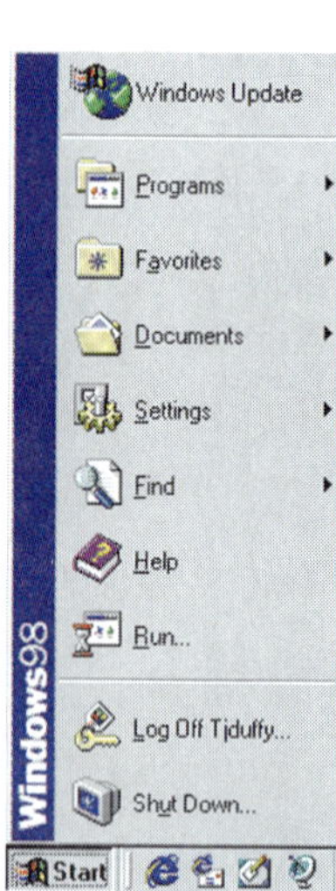

FIGURE 1.14 The Start menu opens when you click the Start button.

6. Close the Recycle Bin window.

Click the Close button at the top of the Recycle Bin window. The Recycle Bin window should now disappear.

7. Open the Start menu.

Click the Start button. The Start menu appears (Figure 1.14). Any menu option with an arrow to the right of it invokes another menu.

8. Open the Programs menu.

Point to the Programs option of the Start menu. A list of menu options starting with Accessories should appear to the right of the Start menu (Figure 1.15). Do not click on any of the menu options.

9. Open the Accessories menu.

Point to the Accessories option with the mouse. The Accessories menu appears (Figure 1.16). Do not click on any of the options.

TIMELY TIP

If you inadvertently activate a program, click on the Close button in the upper-right corner of that application window.

10. Close the Start menu.

Click Click in an unused area of the desktop.

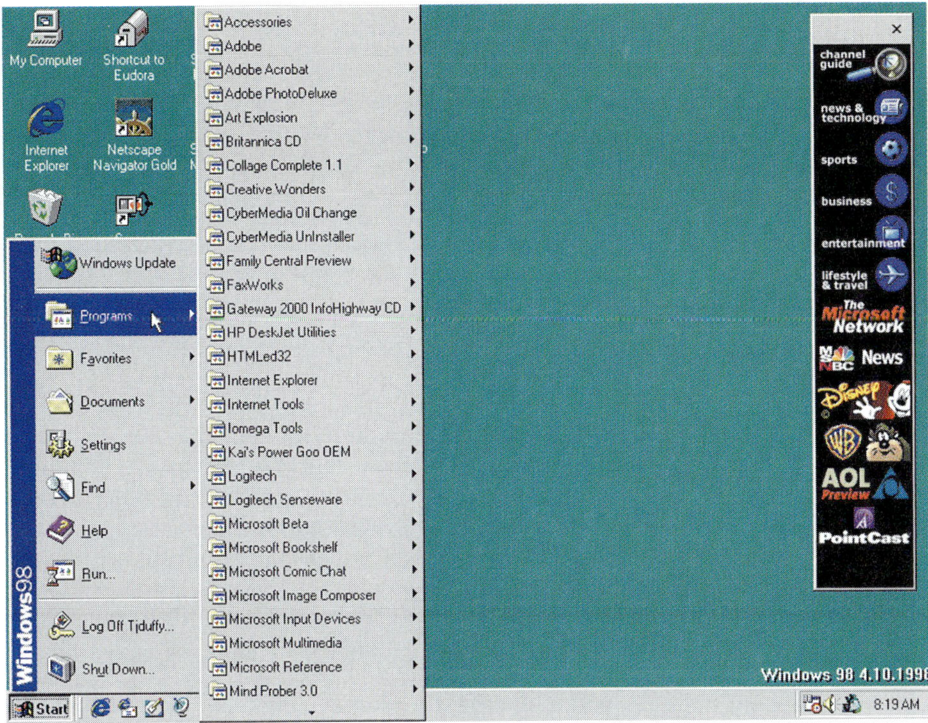

FIGURE 1.15 **The Programs menu.**

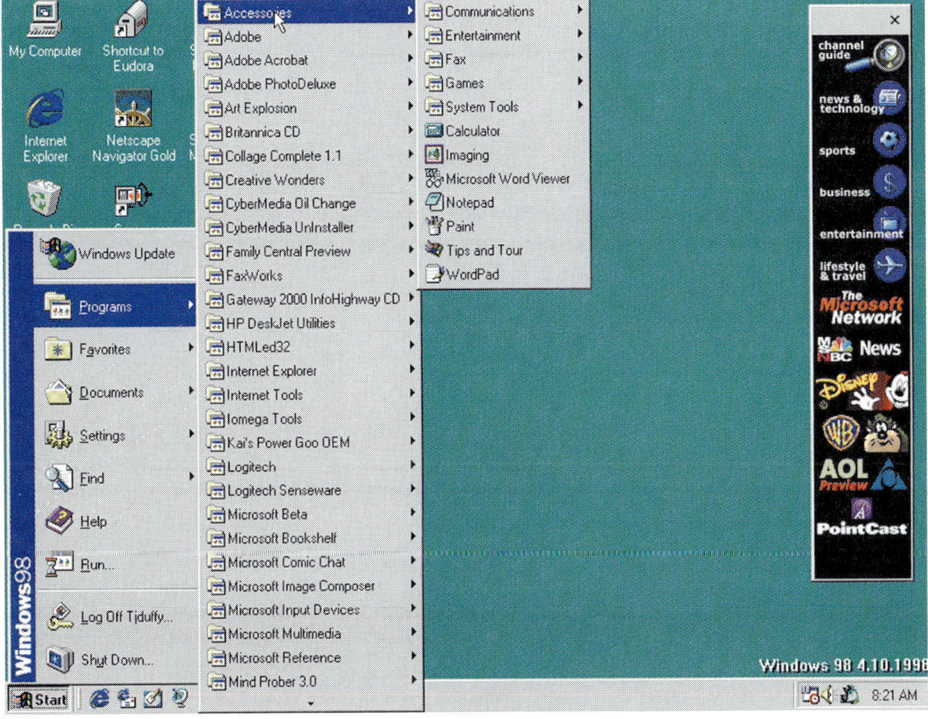

FIGURE 1.16 **The Accessories menu.**

Reinforcing the Exercise

1. The Start button is the starting point for all Windows programs, documents, and settings.
2. When you open a window, an application button icon appears in the taskbar.
3. Documents you delete are stored in the Recycle Bin.
4. The My Computer window gives you information on the various resources of the computer, such as disk drives and printers.

CONTROLLING THE DESKTOP APPEARANCE

If your desktop looks different from that depicted so far in this text, your desktop has probably been configured differently. Windows 98 provides much more control over how your desktop appears and how you interact with that desktop. Windows now refers to the desktop as the **Active Desktop**. Certain features, like the appearance of the Internet Explorer Channel Bar, are automatically installed and included when Windows 98 is initially installed. Other features of the Active Desktop have to be specifically selected.

Displaying the Internet Explorer Channel Bar

The Internet Explorer Channel Bar appears in its own window when it is active. As a result, you can close the window by clicking the Close button in the upper right-hand corner of that window. The Close button appears when you position the mouse to the top of the Channel Bar. Use the commands in the following Hands-On exercise to redisplay the Channel Bar.

Web Options

You can also make your desktop function like World Wide Web applications. This means that each object appears underlined, like an HTML hyperlink, and can be accessed by just clicking the mouse. Web options can be applied using the Folder Options dialog box shown later in Figure 1.23.

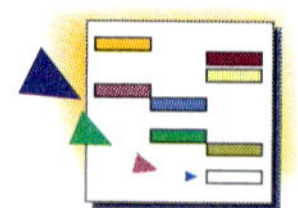

Hands-On Exercise: Manipulating the Channel Bar

1. Close the Channel Bar.

Position the mouse to the top of the Channel Bar (if it is present) and click the Close button of the Internet Explorer Channel Bar.

2. Activate the Channel Bar.

Right-click Right-click a blank area of the Desktop to invoke the context menu.

Active Desktop Choose Active Desktop from the context menu (Figure 1.17).

Customize my Desktop Click on this option to invoke the Display Properties dialog box (Figure 1.18). The dialog box should appear with the Web tab active and the two options shown in Figure 1.18 selected. (If the options are not selected, click each box with the mouse.) These options turn on the Channel Bar and also display the Active Desktop as a Web page.

OK Click the OK button. Your desktop should now appear with the Channel Bar restored.

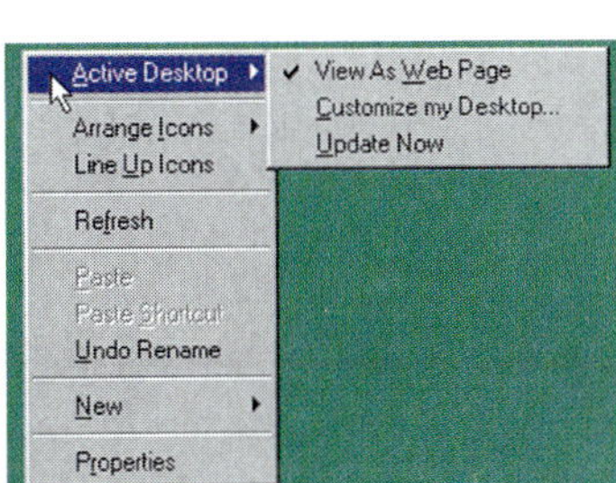

FIGURE 1.17 The context menu options for the Active Desktop.

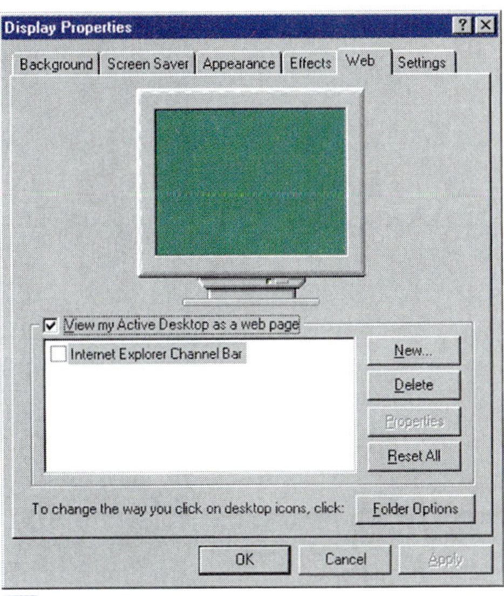

FIGURE 1.18 The Display Properties dialog box.

3. Add a Wallpaper to the Active Desktop.

Right-click Invoke the Context menu by clicking on an unused area of the desktop.

Properties Invoke the Display Properties dialog box. The Background tab should be visible.

Click the down arrow of the Wallpaper list until the Windows 98 option appears. Your Display Properties dialog box should look like Figure 1.19.

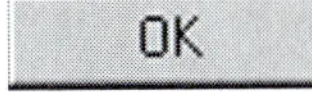

Click the OK button. Your desktop should now appear like that shown in Figure 1.20.

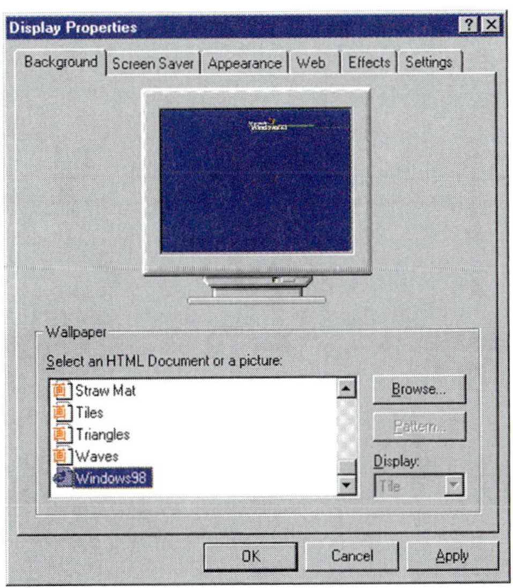

FIGURE 1.19 The Display Properties dialog box with the desired Wallpaper visible.

FIGURE 1.20 **The Active Desktop with the Windows 98 wallpaper applied.**

Reinforcing the Exercise

1. The Close button of the Channel Bar only appears when you position the mouse to the top of the Channel Bar.
2. The Display Properties dialog box is used to control how the desktop appears on the screen.
3. The Background tab of the Display Properties dialog box controls the wallpaper for the desktop.

Timely Tip

The Windows 98 logo that appears at the top of your Active Desktop is actually a Web link that takes you to the Microsoft Windows Update Web page and allows you to check on any Windows 98 updates that might be available. When you click this link, Internet Explorer is automatically started and you are connected to the Internet.

Once you have the Windows 98 wallpaper invoked as your wallpaper for the Web display of the Active Desktop, you can link directly to the Microsoft Web site. You can also add any number of Web-based images and objects to your desktop and customize it in any way that you want. Some of these techniques for trapping objects and images will be covered in the Internet Module of this text. Some computer magazines, for example, contain instructions for creating a "To Do List" that can be placed as wallpaper on your desktop and even allows you to check off those items that you have finished. One disadvantage to such a use, however, is that the list itself cannot be saved easily to disk.

Other Web Characteristics for Windows

You can configure Windows to act just like a Web document. When Windows is configured in this fashion, objects appear like underlined links and require only a single click to start a program, open a folder, or open a document. You can also just indicate to Windows that any windows opened via the My Computer object appear like a Web document. Figure 1.21 shows Web characteristics applied to the Active Desktop. Notice that each shortcut icon is underlined and, as such, requires only a click to activate. Figure 1.22 shows the Web Style applied to the My Computer window. Notice that in addition to showing each of the computer resources as a link, Windows also shows how much space is available in the highlighted item (drive C in this example). Notice also that the mouse pointer has changed to a hand with an extended index finger.

This Web style can be invoked by clicking on the Folders Options button of the Web tab found in the Display Properties dialog box (Figure 1.18). It can also be invoked by clicking on the File Options command of the View menu found in the My Computer window. Either of these options invokes the Folders Options dialog box shown in Figure 1.23.

If you set the Web Style and later want to get rid of it, select the Classic Style. You now are returned to a desktop with a green wallpaper background and no Channel Bar. Use the steps at the beginning of the previous hands-on exercise to set any options that you want to concerning the Desktop.

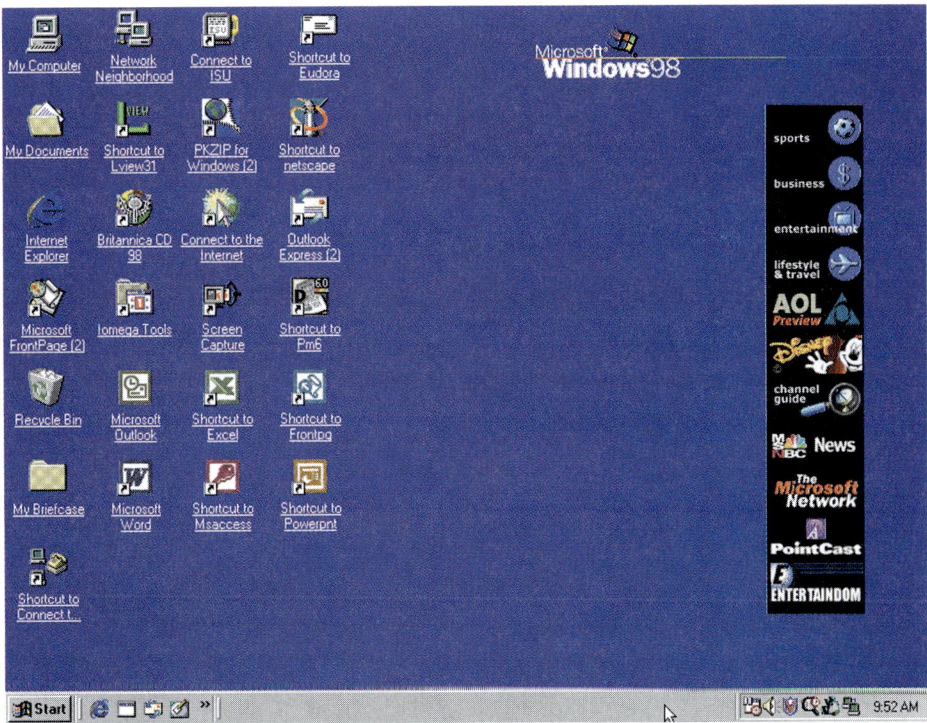

FIGURE 1.21 The Active Desktop with Web characteristics applied to it.

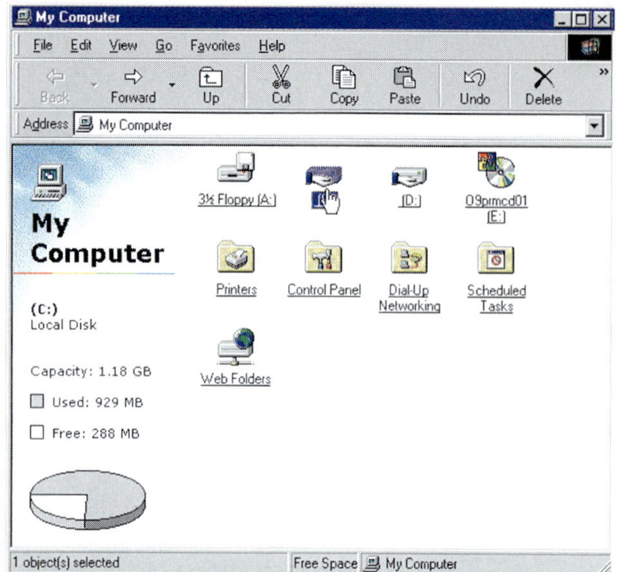

FIGURE 1.22 The My Computer window shown using the Web Style.

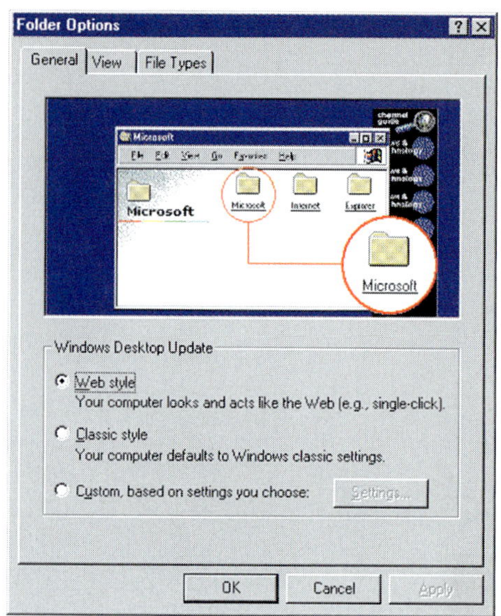

FIGURE 1.23 The File Options dialog box contains options for controlling the display of icons on the Active Desktop.

Hands-On Exercise: Giving My Computer Some Web Characteristics

In this Hands-On Exercise you will be giving some characteristics of the World Wide Web to the display of information displayed in the My Computer window. You will also be manipulating the taskbar and Quick Launch toolbar.

1. Activate the My Computer window.

Double-click to open the My Computer window.

2. Change to Web View.

View Click to invoke the View menu.

As Web Page Click this option. You should now see the My Computer window depicted in Figure 1.24. One advantage of this style is that you receive a visual image of how much storage space is left for any selected disk.

3. Display the storage available for drive C.

Click the drive C icon. You should now see a pie chart like that depicted previously in Figure 1.22 indicating the storage space status for drive C.

4. Click the Printers option and examine the new information displayed in the left-most portion of the My Computer window.

5. Change objects to Web links.

View Click to invoke the View menu.

Folder Options . . . Click to invoke the Folder Options dialog box depicted in Figure 1.23.

O Web Style Click the Web Style button to activate the World Wide Web links feature.

OK Click the OK button to return to the My Computer window. Your screen should now appear similar to that depicted in Figure 1.22.

Close the My Computer window.

6. Move the taskbar.

Click and drag Position the mouse on the middle of the taskbar and use a drag operation to drag it to the right-hand side of the screen. Your desktop should now look like Figure 1.25.

7. Drag the taskbar back to its original location.

TIMELY TIP

Besides moving the taskbar, you can also resize the taskbar via a drag operation so that more options are visible on it.

8. Drag the Quick Launch toolbar off the taskbar.

Click and drag Click to the right of the I-beam of the Quick Launch toolbar and drag it with the 4-headed arrow to a blank area above the taskbar. Your desktop should now look like that depicted in Figure 1.26

9. Return the Quick Launch toolbar to its original location.

TIMELY TIP

A broad vertical I-beam identifies the beginning position of the toolbar. Click to the right of this icon for the drag operation. Use the 4-headed arrow pointer.

FIGURE 1.24 The My Computer window displayed using Web characteristics.

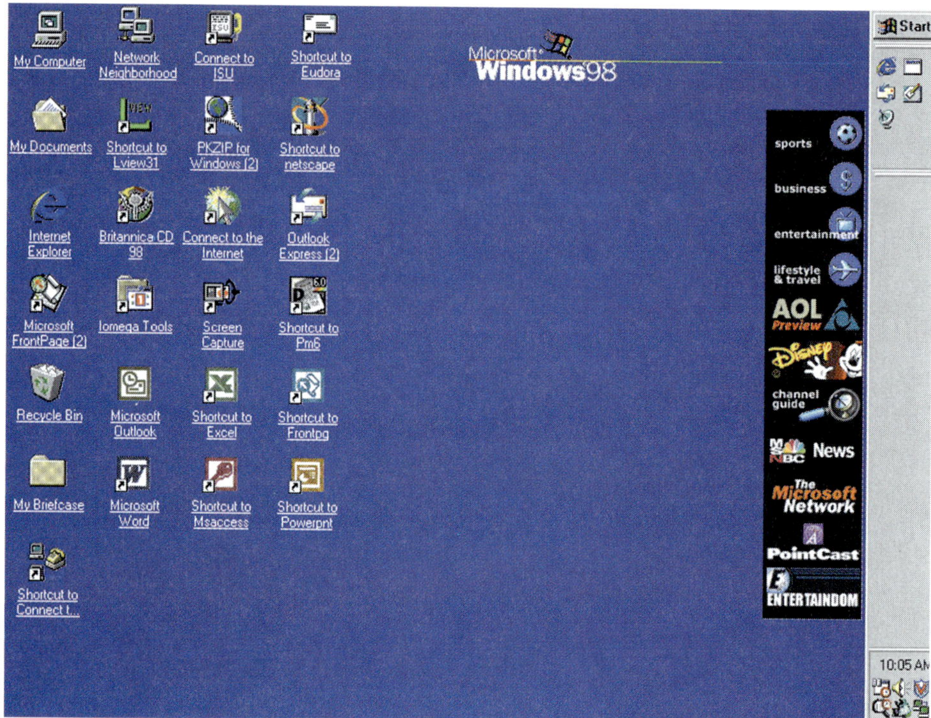

FIGURE 1.25 The taskbar dragged to the right-hand side of the Active Desktop.

FIGURE 1.26 The Quick Launch toolbar moved to its own window.

Reinforcing the Exercise

1. The As Web Page option of the View menu displays additional information about a selected object in the My Computer window.
2. The taskbar can be moved to a different location on the desktop via a drag operation.
3. A toolbar residing on the taskbar can be dragged off the taskbar so it appears in its own window.

On Your Own

Experiment with using the Web Style for examining various resources of your computer. You may want to access drive C to examine some of the items found there.

1. Use the View, Folders Options command sequence to access the Folders Options dialog box and change the method of access to Web Style.
2. After you have had a chance to examine any area of your computer storage that you so desire, use the same commands to change the method of interaction to Classic Style.
3. The Settings button of the Folders Options dialog box allows you to exercise more control over how information gets displayed to the screen (Figure 1.27). For example, you might select to display everything in one window rather than opening a window for each folder.
4. If you mess up, use the methods shown at the beginning of this session to return your Active Desktop back to the desired configuration (start with specifying Classic Style).

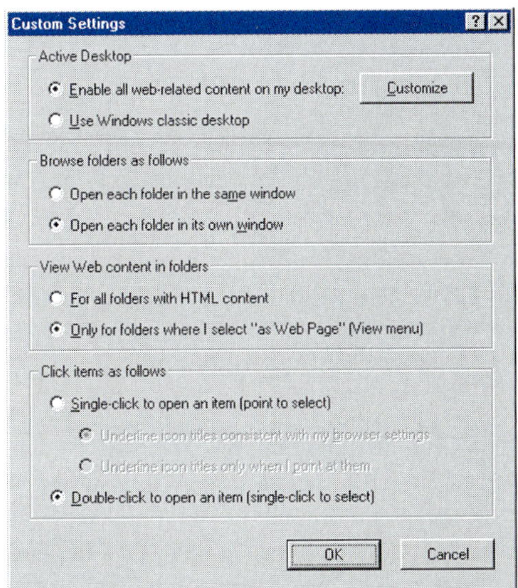

FIGURE 1.27 The Custom Settings dialog box allows you to exercise more control over how objects are displayed to the Active Desktop.

On Your Own

You may have found that what appears on the screen of your monitor does not match in size that which appears in this text's figures. Rather, your images and such appear larger. This is probably because the resolution of your monitor is set at the larger size of 640 by 480 rather than the more commonly used 800 by 600. To set your monitor's resolution to the 800 by 600 setting, issue the following commands. Start, Settings, Control Panel to invoke the Control Panel window. Double-click the Display icon to invoke the Display window. Click the Settings tab. In the lower right-hand corner drag the slider until the resolution is set at 800 by 600.

You should probably wait until after you have finished this chapter and you understand how to interact with windows before attempting this operation.

EXITING WINDOWS

You must be careful to exit Windows properly before you turn off your computer. You should not just turn off the power on your machine while Windows 98 is running. Windows uses many temporary files to perform its tasks and the tasks that you tell it to perform. These temporary files should be closed before you turn off your machine. You use the Shut Down Windows box (Figure 1.28) to close these files properly and exit Windows.

Exiting Windows requires the following steps:

Click the Start button to open the Start menu.

Choose Shut Down from the Start menu. The Shut Down Windows dialog box opens (Figure 1.28). The *Shut down the computer?* option is typically the default.

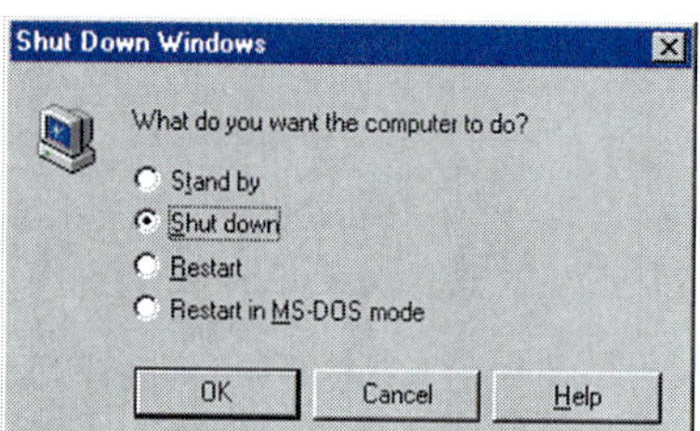

FIGURE 1.28 The Shut Down Windows dialog box provides various options for exiting Windows.

Click the OK button in the Shut Down Windows dialog box. You must wait until the message "It is now safe to turn off your computer" appears in big letters on your screen. Depending on how your computer is set up, you may have to wait several minutes. Once the message appears, you can turn off the computer.

If you are using a computer hooked up to a local area network in a classroom lab, you will probably want to click the *Close all programs and log on as a different user* option. Choosing this option displays a dialog box that the next student will use to log onto Windows. Anything that a subsequent student does on the computer will be traced back to them instead of you.

HANDS-ON EXERCISE: EXITING WINDOWS

1. Go through the steps for properly shutting down the computer.

Click to display the Start menu.

Click to display the Shut Down Windows dialog box. Notice that the *Shut down the computer?* option is automatically selected. If you were truly shutting down your computer, you would now click the Yes button.

2. Return to Windows.

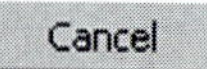

Click to return to Windows.

Reinforcing the Exercise

1. You should properly shut down a computer running Windows or risk damaging temporary files Windows uses to operate.
2. Start the shut down procedure by clicking the Start button.
3. If you are on a network and want to log on, you select *Close all programs and log on as a different user* from the Shut Down Windows box.

PARTS OF A WINDOW

The following sections summarize the parts of a typical window, the My Computer window, shown in Figure 1.29.

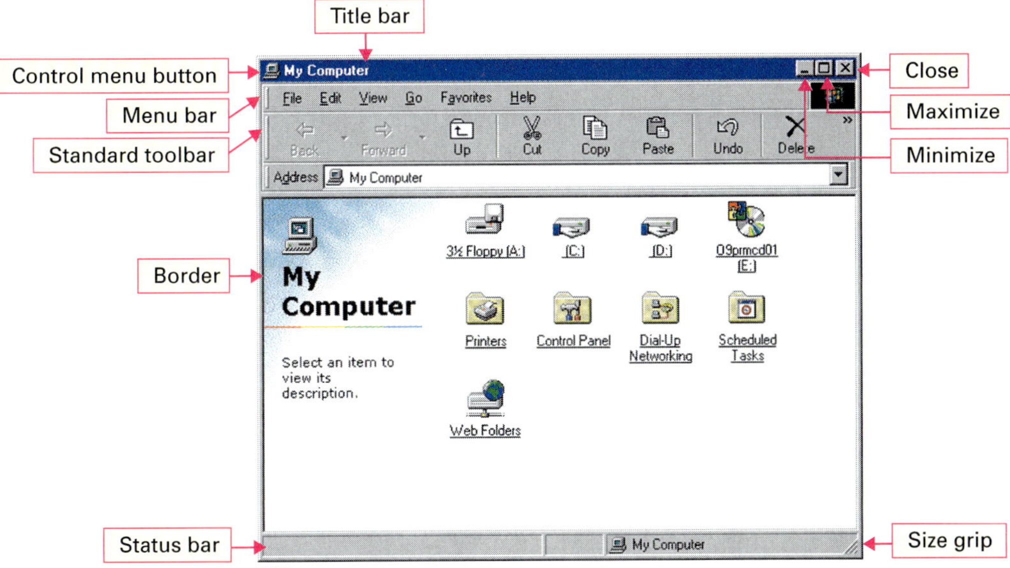

FIGURE 1.29 The parts of the My Computer window.

WINDOW BORDERS

The window **border** shows the limits of the window. You can **resize a window** by using a drag operation on the window border: First you position the pointer on a border line. The pointer turns into a two-headed arrow. You can then drag that border to resize the window.

SIZE GRIP

The **size grip** icon, located in the lower-right corner, is a reference point that you can also use to resize a window easily. When you position the pointer on a size grip, the pointer changes to a double-headed arrow. You can then resize the window with a drag operation.

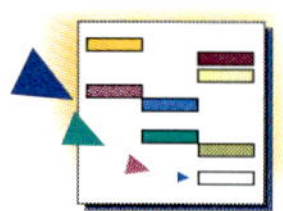

Hands-On Exercise: Changing a Window's Size

1. Open the My Computer window.

Click Position the pointer on the My Computer icon and click the mouse. Your screen should now look similar to Figure 1.29.

2. Make the My Computer window wider.

Drag Position the pointer on the right window border. The pointer should turn into the Horizontal Resize pointer. Drag the border to the right about 1.5 inches.

3. Make the window taller.

Drag Position the pointer on the bottom border of the window. The pointer should turn into the Vertical Resize pointer. Drag the border down about 1 inch.

4. Return the My Computer window back to its original size.

Position the pointer on the size grip in the lower-right corner of the window. The pointer turns into the Diagonal Resize 1 pointer. Drag the size grip up and to the left until the My Computer window is returned to its original size. Leave the My Computer window open for the next part of the discussion.

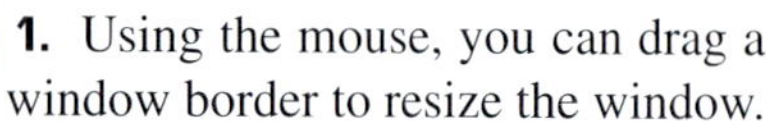

Reinforcing the Exercise

1. Using the mouse, you can drag a window border to resize the window.
2. During a resizing operation, the pointer changes to a double-headed arrow.
3. The icon in the lower-right corner of a window is called the size grip.

Title Bar  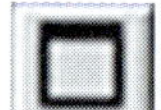  

The top of the window contains a colored bar (typically blue) called the **title bar**. The title bar contains the name of the open application, and four buttons you can use to control the window: the control-menu button, the Minimize button, the Maximize or Restore button, and the Close button.

The **control-menu button** at the left end of the title bar is a throwback to older versions of Windows and is now rarely used. When you click this button, a menu like that shown in Figure 1.30 appears. When you double-click the control-menu button, the window closes (the same as clicking the Close button). Using the Close button (discussed below) instead of the control-menu button is the preferred way to close a window.

When you click an application window's **Minimize button**, the window disappears and only a button representing the application window appears on the taskbar (at the bottom of the desktop). Clicking the **Maximize button** enlarges the window to take up the entire screen. On a window that has been maximized, the Maximize button is replaced by a Restore button. When you click the **Restore button,** the window returns to its previous size. You click the **Close button** to close the application window.

FIGURE 1.30 The control menu appears when you click the control-menu button.

Moving a Window

You can also use the title bar to move a window. This is accomplished by positioning the pointer anywhere in the title bar and then dragging the window to the desired location.

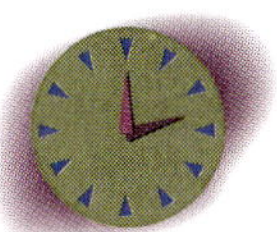

Timely Tip

What if you have used the Minimize button to reduce an application window to a button on the taskbar and you want to get rid of that button? You must first open the application by clicking the appropriate taskbar button. When the application window appears, you can click the Close button of that application window to close it, and the button for that application disappears from the taskbar.

Scroll Bar

A window may also have a **scroll bar** on the border (Figure 1.30). When you click on an arrow button, the screen moves in that direction. The position of the **scroll box** indicates the location of the cursor in the displayed text. You can drag the scroll box slider to move quickly from one part of the screen to another. Clicking around the scroll box slider moves the information one screen at a time.

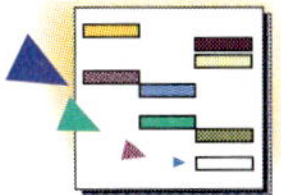

Hands-On Exercise: Using Title Bar Features

The My Computer window should still appear on the Windows desktop.

1. Maximize the window.

Click to make the My Computer window take up the entire desktop. Notice that if you let your mouse pointer rest over the button a ToolTip appears identifying the button.

2. Restore the window to its original size.

Click to return the My Computer window to its original size.

3. Minimize the My Computer window to a button on the taskbar.

Click so that the only evidence of the My Computer window is a button on the taskbar.

4. Open the My Computer window by clicking on that taskbar button.

Click to reopen the window.

5. Move the window.

Position the pointer anywhere in the title bar of the My Computer window, and drag down and to the lower-right corner. The window moves with the pointer.

6. Drag the window back to its prior location.

Reinforcing the Exercise

1. Once a window is maximized, the Restore button replaces the Maximize button in the title bar.
2. To move a window on the desktop, you click anywhere in the title bar and drag the window.
3. When you click the Minimize button, the window is reduced to a button on the taskbar.
4. The recommended (and easiest) way to close a window is to click the Close button at the right end of the title bar.

Menu Bar

The **menu bar** gives you access to the commands you need to work within the window. Windows is consistent in how menus are arranged and in what types of commands, or options, are used in the menus from application to application. This consistency of menu display and use makes different Windows applications easier to learn.

You can open a menu from the menu bar by clicking the menu name. For example, when you click View in the menu bar, the View menu opens with a set of options for you to choose from (Figure 1.31). The menus you open from the menu bar are often called **pull-down menus**. You issue a command through a pull-down menu by clicking the appropriate option, by typing the letter that is underlined in the option name, or by using the arrow keys to highlight the option and then pressing Enter. When you choose an option that has a right arrow by its name, like Arrange Icons in the View menu, a new cascading menu opens (Figure 1.32). When you choose a menu option that has an **ellipsis** (. . .) by its name, a dialog box appears (Figure 1.33). Table 1.4 lists the meanings of the symbols and conventions used in Windows menus.

Alternatively, you can select menu options by typing **keyboard shortcut commands**. For example, the shortcut command that opens the View menu is ALT + V (the underlined letter). Although you can issue shortcut commands from the keyboard, most computer novices find them cumbersome and difficult to memorize initially. Since Windows and applications that run in Windows are designed to be used with the mouse, you will primarily use the mouse in this text.

Timely Tip

In this text, a series of menu selections is called a **command sequence**. For example, you invoke the View, Arrange Icons command sequence by first choosing View from the menu bar and then choosing Arrange Icons from the View menu.

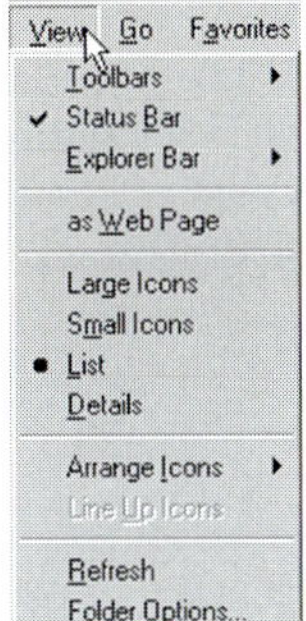

FIGURE 1.31 The View pull-down menu.

If you open a menu and then decide that you don't want to do anything with that particular menu, you can open an adjacent menu using the right or left arrow key or by clicking with the mouse. If you want to close a menu, position the pointer anywhere outside that menu and click, or press (ESC) one or more times.

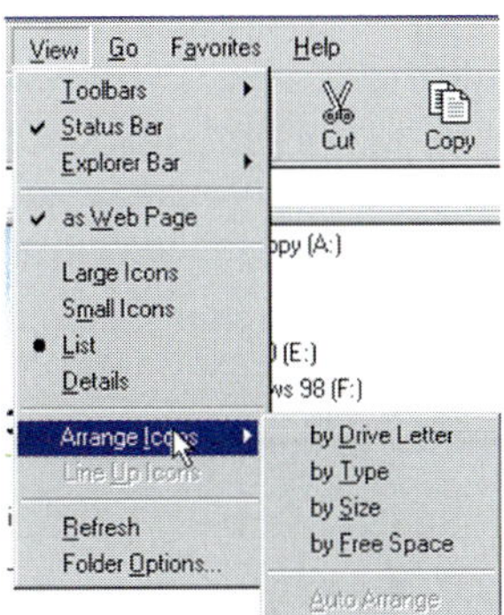

FIGURE 1.32 The new cascading menu opened by choosing Arrange Icons from the View menu.

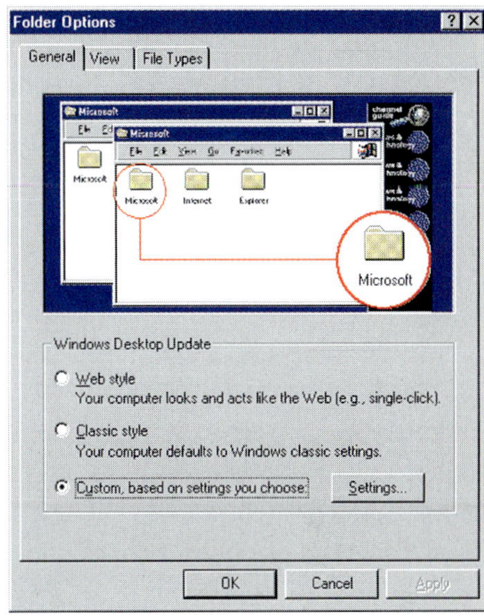

FIGURE 1.33 The Folder Options dialog box.

TABLE 1.4 Meanings of Symbols and Conventions Used in Windows Menus

Description	Appearance	Meaning
Ellipsis	...	A dialog box will appear when you select this command option. The dialog box contains additional options for this command.
Dimmed entry	Auto Arrange	This command option is not available at this time. You have to enter a previous command before this one becomes available.
Checkmark	✔	This command option is in effect. Selecting this command again disables the command and removes the checkmark. More than one of this type of option can be activated.
Dot	●	This command option is in effect. Selecting this command again disables the command and removes the large dot. This differs from the check mark in that only one of these options can be activated at a time.
Keys	(CTRL) + Z	A key combination (such as (CTRL) + Z) is a shortcut command for this particular option.
Right triangle	▶	An additional menu of options will appear when you select this option command.

Standard Toolbar

The **Standard Toolbar** on the My Computer window contains buttons for commonly used commands. Clicking on a button to execute a command is usually faster than using a menu sequence of commands to execute a common command. Table 1.5 shows each button and its function.

TABLE 1.5 The Standard Toolbar of the My Computer Window

Button	Button Name	Description
Back	Back	Displays the previous window accessed using My Computer (available only if the single window option is used).
Forward	Forward	Displays the next window in a series accessed via My Computer (available only if the single window option is used). The down arrow on both of these buttons displays a listing of resources accessed via various windows. Clicking an item displayed, displays the contents of that window.
Up	Up	Moves up one level in the structure examined using My Computer (discussed in more detail in Session 3).
Cut	Cut	Used to move items from one window to another.
Copy	Copy	Used to copy items from one window to another.
Paste	Paste	Used to complete a copy or move operation.
Undo	Undo	Used to reverse an operation that was just performed.
Delete	Delete	Used to delete items from the window.
Properties	Properties	Used to display the Properties dialog box for the selected object.
Views	View	Used to control how items are displayed in the window.

Address Box

The Address Box is used to open Web pages, programs, folders, or documents. It shows the current location (Web page or folder).

Timely Tip

If you do not see one of the items discussed above, issue the View, Toolbars command sequence. From the Toolbars submenu, select the desired item to display it. It should be noted that the Text Labels entry must be selected before the status bar operates as indicated in the following discussion.

Status Bar

The **status bar** at the bottom of the window provides information on the item you select. The status bar does not appear on every window. If you select an object, for example, you may see information on the number of objects selected and the amount of free space on the disk. Descriptive information about menu items also appears in this area.

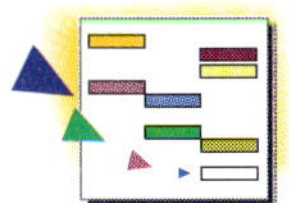

Hands-On Exercise: Using Menus

The My Computer window should be visible on the desktop. If it isn't, click on the icon to open the window.

1. Use the mouse to open menus.

View Click this menu bar option to open the View pull-down menu (Figure 1.31).

Timely Tip

Throughout this text, the following system is used to show how keystrokes (if covered) are combined. When two or three keystrokes are separated by addition signs (such as CTRL + DEL), you must hold down the first key while you press the additional key or keys. When two keystrokes are separated by a comma (such as F2, DEL), simply press and release each key in the order given.

2. Open the Arrange Icons menu. The arrow to the right of the Arrange Icons option indicates a cascading menu will appear.

Arrange Icons Click to display the Arrange Icons menu (Figure 1.32).

Click Click any unused area of the window to exit the menu.

3. Open the Edit menu.

Edit Click to display this menu bar option. The Edit pull-down menu appears (Figure 1.34)

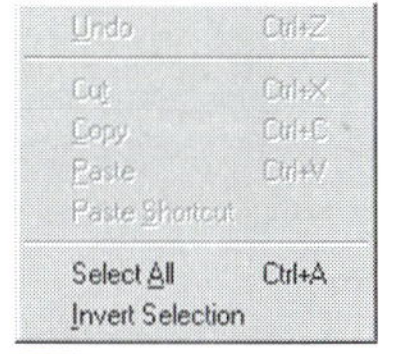

FIGURE 1.34
The Edit menu.

Click Click any unused area of the My Computer window to exit the menu.

4. Open a menu using a shortcut command.

ALT + F Press this key combination to open the File pull-down menu (Figure 1.35).

5. Open the View pull-down menu.

→ (twice) Press the right arrow twice to open the View menu.

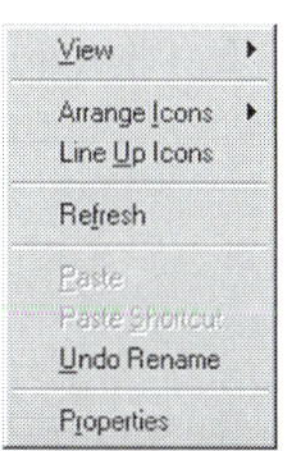

FIGURE 1.35
The File menu opened by issuing the ALT + F shortcut command.

6. Manually exit the menu.

ESC Pressing ESC once closes the View menu. On the menu bar, the View option is still selected (Figure 1.36)—the menu options still appear as a button.

ESC Pressing ESC again returns control back to the My Computer window.

7. Open a dialog box.

View Click this menu bar option to open the View menu.

Folder Options . . . Click this View menu option to open the Folder Options dialog box. The General tab should be on top. If it isn't, click it to activate it.

View Click to activate the View tab (Figure 1.37). Notice how the dialog box has changed to reflect the appearance of the active tab page.

Cancel Click the Cancel button of the Folder Options dialog box.

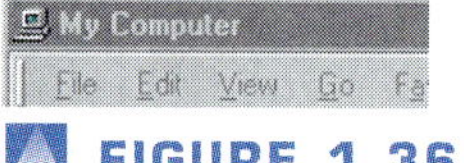

FIGURE 1.36 **After you press ESC once, File is still selected (appears as a button) on the menu bar.**

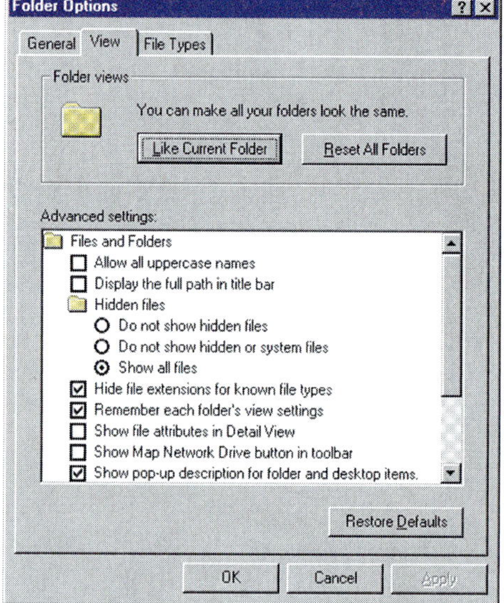

FIGURE 1.37 **The Folder Options dialog box with the View tab active.**

Reinforcing the Exercise

1. You can open a menu from the menu bar by clicking its name or by pressing ALT + the letter in its name that is underlined.
2. You close a menu by clicking anywhere on the window outside of the menu or by pressing ESC several times.
3. An ellipsis after an option name indicates that a dialog box will open when you select that option.
4. A right arrow after an option name indicates that another menu will open when you select that option.

Using Windows Dialog Boxes

As mentioned in the discussion of menus, a **dialog box** automatically appears on-screen after you select a menu option that has an ellipsis (. . .). For example, selecting the Folder Options option from the View menu opens the dialog box. A dialog box is a window that prompts you for information it needs to carry out a command. A dialog box may, like the Options dialog box, have tabs that when clicked display a different part of the dialog box. In Figure 1.37, the View tab is active.

A dialog box also contains controls. **Controls** allow you to interact with a dialog box or window. Common types of controls include text boxes, check boxes, list boxes, option buttons, command buttons, spin boxes, and various combinations of these elements. Figure 1.38 shows the Print dialog box with each of these controls labeled.

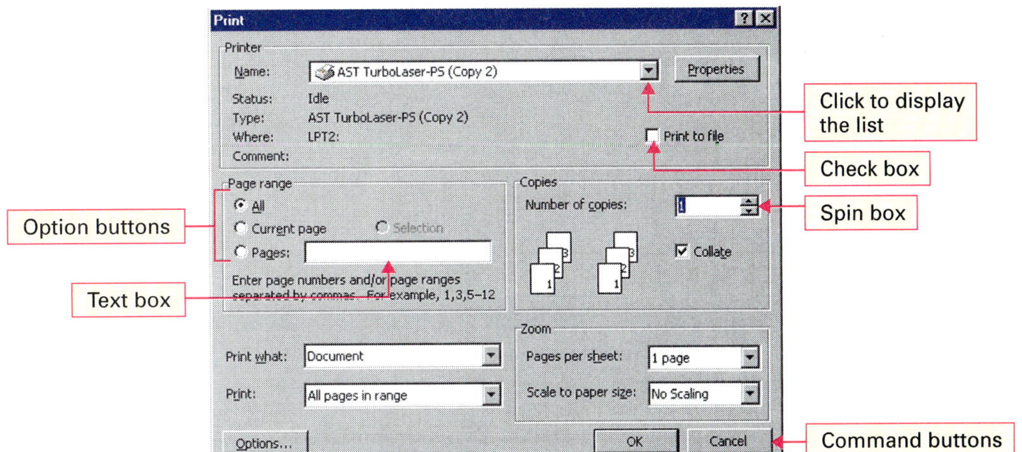

FIGURE 1.38 Word's Print dialog box contains a number of controls.

Option Buttons

Option buttons turn options on or off. Only one option button can be on at once. A dot ( ) next to an option shows which option button is selected.

List Boxes

A **list box** displays a list of options from which you can choose. To see the list, you may have to click the down arrow at the right end of the box. To select an option, you click it. If there are more items than will fit in the box, a scroll bar will appear on the right side of the list box to allow you to move through the list.

Check Boxes

A **check box** turns an option on and off. A check ( ) in a check box means the option is on. Several check boxes can be active at one time. To check or uncheck an item, you click it.

Command Buttons

You issue commands by clicking **command buttons** in an open dialog box. Two common command buttons are OK and Cancel. OK confirms choices and closes the dialog box. Cancel ignores any choices that you made and closes the dialog box. A command button with an ellipsis (. . .) after its name takes you to another dialog box.

Text Boxes

A **text box** allows you to enter and edit information that is needed to perform a task, such as entering the name of a file. A text box may include the insertion point when the dialog box opens, or you can place the insertion point there by clicking inside the text box.

Spin Boxes

A **spin box** is a control with a number and small up and down arrow icons to the right of the box. You click these arrows to increase or decrease the value contained in the spin box. If you do not want to use the incremental approach, you can type the desired number directly in the spin box text field.

Hands-On Exercise: Using Dialog Boxes

1. Close the My Computer window and start Word.

Start — Click the Start button. The Start menu appears.

Programs — Point to this option to open the Programs menu.

Microsoft Word — Click to start Microsoft Word (Figure 1.39). Your screen might look slightly different.

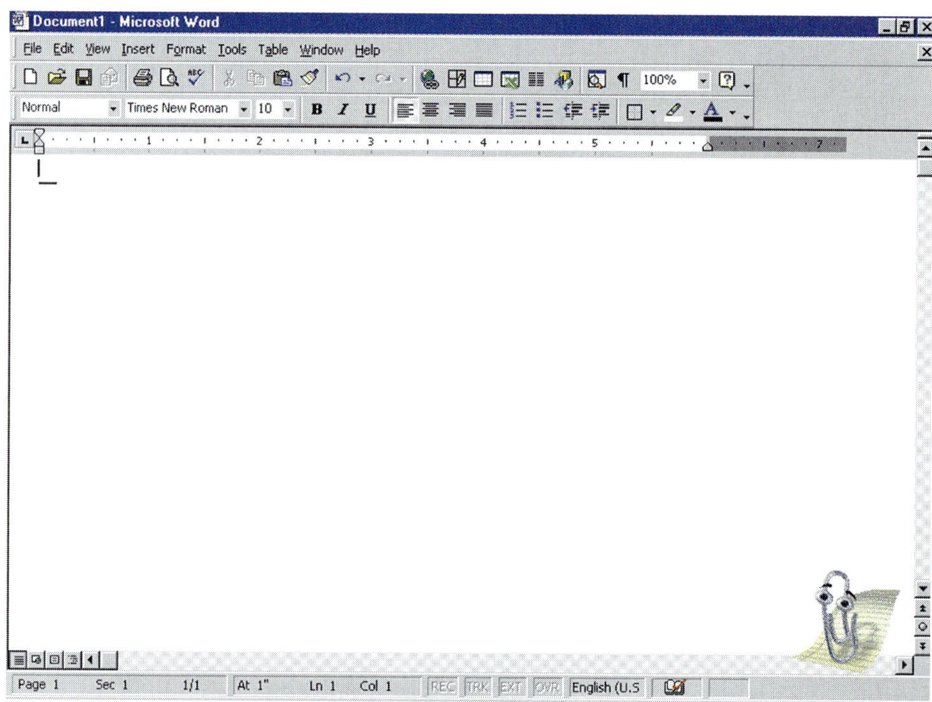

FIGURE 1.39 The Microsoft Word window.

2. Open the Print dialog box.

File — Click to open the File menu.

Print . . . — Click to open the Print dialog box (Figure 1.40). Your Print dialog box will probably look different.

3. Use the Copies spin box to determine the number of copies.

Use the up arrow of the spin box to increase the number of copies to 6 (Figure 1.41).

Use the down arrow of the spin box to reset the number of copies back to 1.

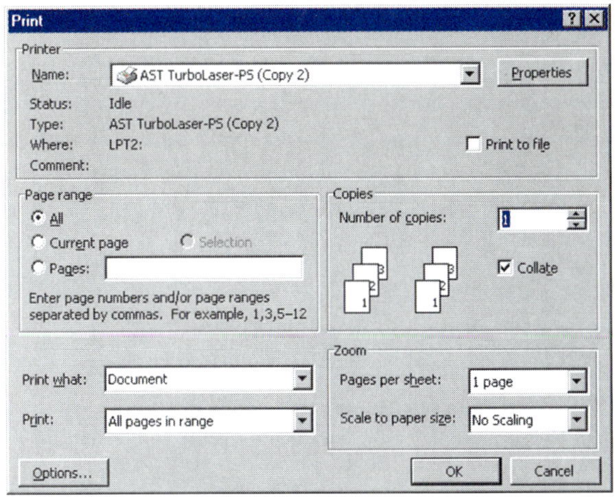

FIGURE 1.40 Word's Print dialog box.

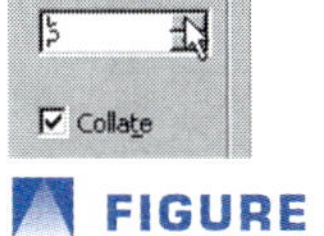

FIGURE 1.41 The spin box with the contents of 6.

4. Use the Option button.

Pages Click to change the selection. Notice that All is no longer selected. Remember, when you are using option buttons, only one button can be active at any one time.

All Click to change the selection. Again, only one remains selected.

5. Use a text box.

Pages Click to change the selection.

Type: 4 The number 4 should now appear in the Pages text box (Figure 1.42).

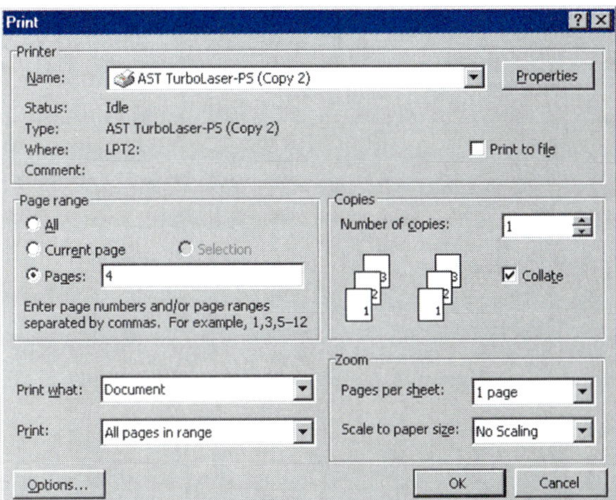

FIGURE 1.42 The Pages text box now contains a value of 4.

6. Select from a selection box.

Print what Point to the Print what list box. The current selection is Document.

Click to display a list of options (Figure 1.43).

Styles Select "Styles" from the drop-down list box.

7. Use a command button to exit the dialog box.

Cancel Click the cancel button to return to the application window.

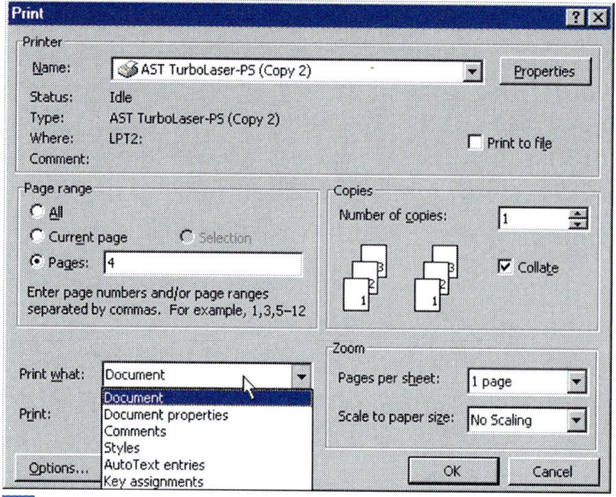

FIGURE 1.43 The Print what list box offers several alternatives of what to print.

8. Return to the desktop.

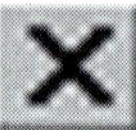

Click the Close button on the Microsoft Word title bar.

Reinforcing the Exercise

1. You use a dialog box to provide Windows with the additional information it needs to complete a command.
2. The spin box is a dialog box control that has arrows that allow you to change its value or you can type in the new value.
3. In a dialog box, only one option button can be active at one time.
4. Use the Cancel button to exit a dialog box without saving changes.
5. You can use more than one check box.
6. Command buttons typically allow you to accept or cancel any changes that have been made to a dialog box.
7. A list box provides alternatives from which you can make a selection.
8. A text box allows you to enter something.

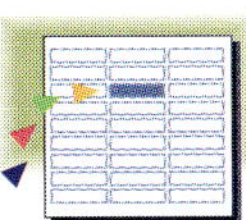

On Your Own

Windows 98 provides the ability to control how you interact with Windows by providing the ability to not only configure the Start menu to your requirements but also by displaying various toolbars on the taskbar. Windows 98 provides three additional toolbars that can be part of the taskbar. These toolbars are accessed by right clicking the mouse on the taskbar and then selecting the Toolbars entry. These toolbar options of the context menu can be seen in Figure 1.44.

Windows also allows you to easily edit the Start menu. Dragging an item off the Start menu or any submenu removes the item from the menu. To leave items on the Start menu and create shortcuts for the item on the desktop, you will want to copy the Start menu item as you drag it to the desktop. You can drag Start menu items to the desktop or to an open dialog box or folder while holding down the CTRL key. When you are holding down the CTRL key, the mouse pointer appears with a plus sign (+) to indicate that you are copying the icon.

1. Experiment with the various toolbars that can be added to the taskbar using the context menu. See what type of impact they have on the appearance of the taskbar.
2. Open several windows and explore the various windows options that appear on the taskbar's context menu.
3. Copy the WordPad menu option from the Accessories cascading menu to the desktop as a shortcut. Be sure to hold down the CTRL key while you are doing this. Make certain that the WordPad icon still resides in the Accessories menu. If you mess up, and delete the WordPad icon from the Accessories menu, just drag it back to the correct location.
4. Delete the WordPad icon from your desktop by right-clicking the mouse to invoke the context menu and select Delete.
5. Try to restore this shortcut that you have deleted using the Recycle Bin.
6. Add any other icons that you wish to use as shortcuts to the desktop.

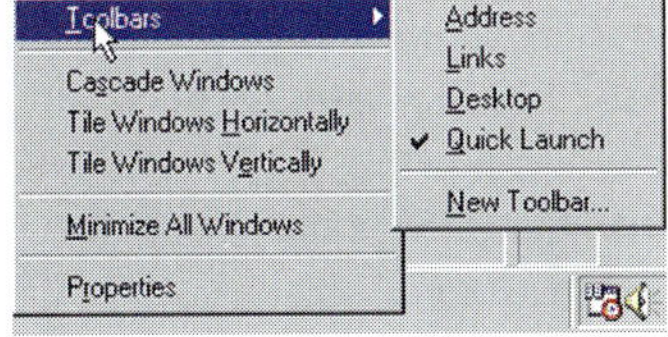

FIGURE 1.44 The available toolbar options in the taskbar context menu.

Session Review

Windows 98 automatically starts when you turn on your computer. If your computer is connected to a network, you may have to log onto the network via a Windows dialog box.

Windows uses a graphical user interface (GUI) that allows you to enter commands easily, either by using a mouse as a pointing tool or by entering commands from the keyboard. Once you start Windows, you invoke commands by using objects from the desktop. The desktop may contain more than one window. The active window is on top with a colored title bar. Some commands may also require you to enter some additional information in dialog boxes.

The Windows interface uses graphic images called icons to represent applications or objects. Using the Minimize button, you can also reduce an application to a button on the taskbar. To reopen the application, you click on its taskbar button.

Application windows can be either active or inactive. An active window is the top window with the colored title bar; any other windows are inactive. Only an active window can have commands executed in it. An inactive window can be activated by clicking on any part of that window or clicking its corresponding button in the taskbar.

Windows 98 makes use of a feature called the Active Desktop. This allows you to change the desktop so that it conforms to your exact wishes. For example, you can change it so that items appear underlined and can be selected with a single click, just as on the

Web. You can also exercise control over how the task bar appears on the screen and which toolbars appear on it.

You can resize any window by using the Maximize, Minimize, and Restore buttons. You can also resize them by using the mouse to drag window borders. The pointer changes shape to show the direction of the resizing operation.

The easiest way to close a window is by clicking the Close button on the title bar. You also can close a window by double-clicking the control-menu button.

Windows makes extensive use of menus. Menu options represent commands. When you select an option on the menu bar, a pull-down menu appears with more options to choose from. Many commands, called shortcut commands, can also be executed by using the keyboard rather than a menu.

Many commands also invoke dialog boxes. A dialog box serves to provide Windows with more information about what exactly is desired by the user in executing a particular command.

The taskbar can be repositioned to any side of the desktop using a drag operation. In addition, a number of toolbars can be made to appear on the taskbar using its context menu.

Key Terms and Concepts

Active Desktop 16
active window 11
border 25
check box 33
click 4
Close button 26
command button 33
command sequence 28
context menu 4
control-menu button 26
controls 33
deselect 4
desktop 2
dialog box 32
disk operating system (DOS) 2
double-click 4
drag 4
ellipsis 28
graphical user interface (GUI) 1
icon 3
inactive window 11
Internet Explorer Channel Bar 9
keyboard shortcut command 3, 28
list box 33
Maximize button 26
menu bar 28
Minimize button 26
mouse 1
multitasking 11
My Computer 8
object 3
operating system 1
option button 33
Outlook Express 9
Point 4
property 3
pull-down menu 28
Recycle Bin 9
resize a window 25
Restore button 26
right-click 4
scroll bar 27
scroll box 27
size grip 25
spin box 33
Standard toolbar 30
Start button 10
status area/system tray 9
status bar 31
taskbar 9
text box 33
title bar 26
toolbar 10
ToolTip 8

Session Quiz

Multiple Choice

1. Which of the following objects provides information about your computer's resources?
   - **a.** inbox
   - **b.** taskbar
   - **c.** My Computer
   - **d.** Network Neighborhood
2. What is the term used by Windows to indicate the whole screen?
   - **a.** macro window
   - **b.** dialog box
   - **c.** desktop or Active Desktop
   - **d.** active window

3. Which of the following buttons can reduce an application to a button on the taskbar?
   a. Maximize
   b. control-menu
   c. Minimize
   d. Restore
4. The process of having multiple applications open and available for use at one time is called:
   a. windowing
   b. multitasking
   c. multiprocessing
   d. multiple windows
5. Which of the following statement(s) about the active desktop is(are) true?
   a. You can activate the Help feature by pressing the F2 key.
   b. The Internet Explorer Channel Bar is usually part of the Active Desktop when it is viewed as a Web page.
   c. When using the Active Desktop items are automatically placed in underlined, Web format.
   d. The Folders Options dialog box is used to activate the Active Desktop Web mode.

True/False

6. A window that resides beneath another window is an active window.
7. You can enter Windows commands only by using a mouse or trackball.
8. You can activate a minimized application by clicking that application's button on the taskbar.
9. Clicking and dragging the title bar of a window resizes that window.
10. The Windows pointer changes shape depending on the task being performed.

Session Review Exercises

1. Define or describe each of the following:
   a. My Computer
   b. active window
   c. desktop
   d. taskbar
2. A shortcut or context menu can be activated by clicking the __________ button of the mouse.
3. The __________ __________ option of the context menu controls how the desktop appears visually on your computer screen.
4. The __________ __________ icon opens a window that allows you to examine the available computer resources.
5. The acronym GUI means __________ __________ __________ .
6. The pointing device most frequently used with Windows is the __________ .
7. The entire Windows screen is called the __________ .
8. Pressing and releasing the mouse button is called __________ .
9. Holding down the mouse button and moving the mouse is called __________ .
10. The __________ button on the taskbar opens a menu that can lead you through a whole series of menus.
11. Allowing the pointer to rest over an icon displays a __________ explaining that icon's function.
12. The __________ button is used to shrink an application window to a button on the taskbar.
13. Clicking the __________ button closes an application window.
14. An __________ after a pull-down menu option indicates that if this command is selected a dialog box will appear on the screen.
15. The __________ button changes a maximized window back to its original size.
16. The __________ bar is used to move quickly through text or information contained in a window or selection box.
17. The __________ __________ dialog box controls how folders and files are displayed using the Active Desktop.
18. The active window is always the __________ window on the screen.
19. If you don't like the location of the taskbar it can be __________ to a new location on the screen.
20. An icon represented by a Web linked is accessed by __________ the mouse.

Computer Exercises

1. Practice using the mouse.
   a. Click the Start button, and then open the Programs, Accessories, and Games menus.
   b. Select the game Solitaire.
   c. Play one game of Solitaire to practice clicking and dragging.
   d. Close the Solitaire window.

2. Practice opening and closing Windows applications.
   a. Start and exit two or three Windows applications. Be sure to use the Close button, or choose Exit from the File option of the menu bar to close an application.
   b. Close any application window when you are finished.
   c. Open Excel. Click its Restore button. Open Word. Click its Restore button. You should now have a screen that looks something like Figure 1.45. Maximize the first window and close it using the Close button. Do the same for the remaining window.
   d. Close the window.

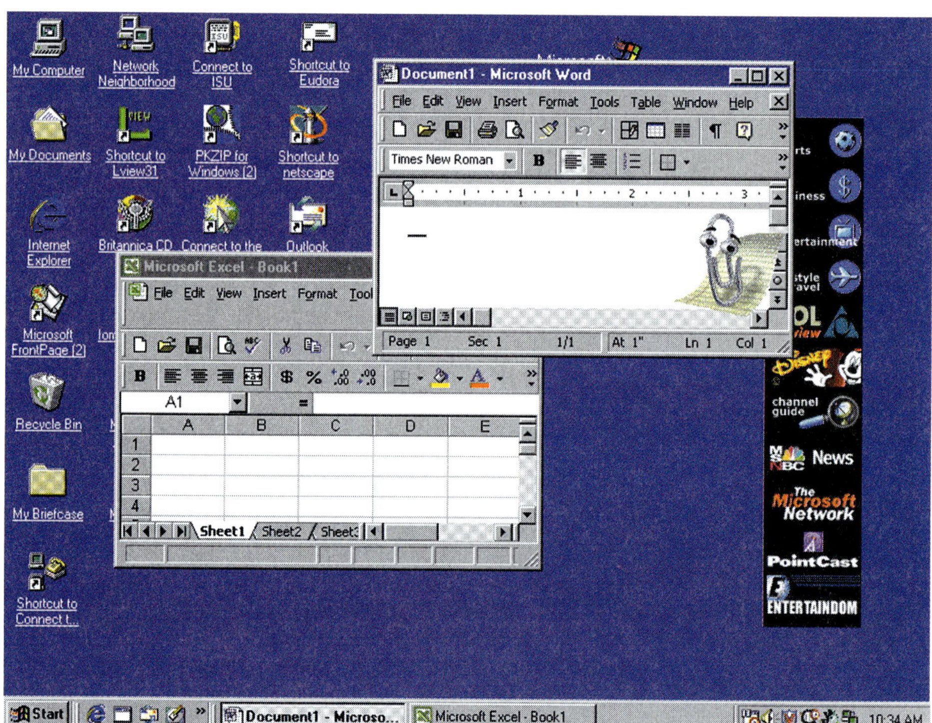

FIGURE 1.45
The Windows desktop with the Excel and Word windows both visible.

3. Practice changing the size of the My Computer window.
   a. Open the My Computer window if it is not open.
   b. Open the My Computer window.
   c. Maximize the My Computer window.
   d. Restore the My Computer window to its previous size.
   e. Close the window.

4. Practice activating and using various accessory programs.
   a. Click the Start button, and point to Programs and then Accessories. From the Accessories menu, activate the Paint program.
   b. Using the mouse and the various drawing buttons along the left and bottom borders, experiment with the Paint application.
   c. Minimize the Paint window to a taskbar icon.
   d. Activate the Calculator from the Accessories menu.

        1) Perform the following calculations:
           1945/235_______
           125*4535_______
           1281+2341+2871+7655___________
        2) Reduce the Calculator to a taskbar button.
   e. Activate the Paint program by using its taskbar button.
   f. Activate the Calculator program by using its taskbar button.
   g. Click the Close button of the Calculator window to close it.
   h. Click the Close button of the Paint window to close it. Answer No when requested about saving any changes.
5. Open three programs from the Accessories submenu.
   a. If necessary, click the Restore button to reduce the size of application windows that take up the whole screen.
   b. Drag and resize the windows so that you can see parts of all three application windows.
   c. From an unused area of the taskbar, invoke the taskbar context menu. Examine the effect that the following commands have:
        1) Cascade Windows
        2) Tile Windows Horizontally
        3) Tile Windows Vertically
        4) Minimize All Windows
6. If you have your own computer, experiment with controlling your desktop. Configure it with features that most appeal to you. If you mess up issue the View, Folder Options command sequence and select the Classic Style option. You can then start the process over.

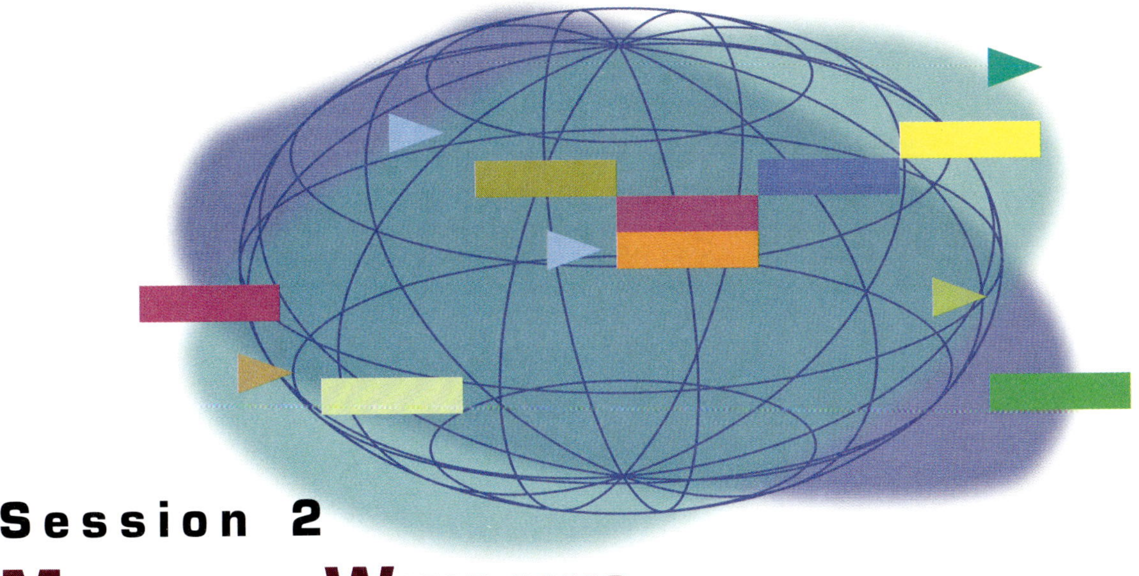

Session 2
More on Windows

After completing this session, you should be able to:

- Utilize the clipboard
- Use the Paint program
- Use the Copy command
- View information on the clipboard
- Use the Windows Help feature

THE WINDOWS CLIPBOARD

Windows contains an object called the **clipboard** that allows you to copy text or graphics from one application to another. The Windows clipboard is an area in memory that an application uses to store data temporarily during a cut, paste, or copy operation.

A **Copy command** occurs when a likeness of data is placed in the clipboard, leaving the original data unchanged. The **Cut command** removes the data from its original location and places it in the clipboard. The **Paste command** copies data from the clipboard and places it in a document.

The clipboard can only handle data from one Cut or Copy command at a time. Data in the clipboard is destroyed and replaced when a subsequent Cut or Copy command is issued. Using a Paste command leaves the data in the clipboard unchanged. You will use the clipboard in the following Hands-On Exercise involving the Windows drawing program, Paint.

Timely Tip

You can use the following keyboard shortcut commands instead of menu sequences for the Copy, Cut, and Paste commands:

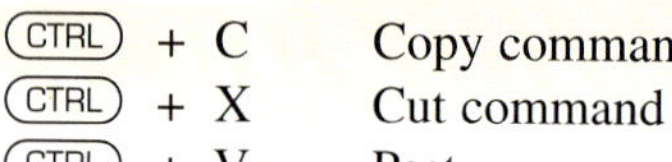

CTRL + C Copy command
CTRL + X Cut command
CTRL + V Paste command
CTRL + Z Undo command

THE PAINT PROGRAM

Windows contains a built-in program called **Paint** that allows you to do freehand drawing. You can use this program to draw just about anything that you want. Table 2.1 shows the tool box buttons that appear in the Paint window and what you can do with them. Using this program allows you to reinforce a number of different mouse commands.

TABLE 2.1 Paint Tool Box Buttons

Button	Name	Allows You To:
	Free-Form Select	Select irregular-shaped areas of the image for a move, copy, or edit
	Select	Initiate a drag operation to select a rectangular area of the image for a move, copy, or edit
	Eraser/Color/Eraser	Selectively erase parts of the image
	Fill With Color	Fill a delimited area with the selected color from the palette
	Pick Color	Select a colored area of an image to copy to another part of the image
	Magnifier	Enlarge an area of the image a selected amount
	Pencil	Draw a line one pixel (dot) wide
	Brush	Draw or create an image
	Airbrush	Airbrush the image
	Text	Label parts of the image
	Line	Draw a line of a selected thickness
	Curve	Draw a curve of a selected thickness

TABLE 2.1 Paint Tool Box Buttons (continued)

Button	Name	Allows You To:
	Rectangle	Draw a rectangle with a selected fill style
	Polygon	Draw a polygon with a selected fill style
	Ellipse	Draw an ellipse with a selected fill style
	Rounded Rectangle	Draw a rounded rectangle with a selected fill style

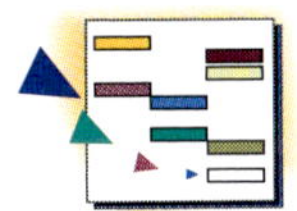

Hands-On Exercise: Using the Paint Program

1. Start the Paint application.

Click the Start button. The Start menu appears.

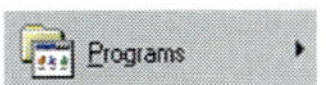

Point to this option to open the Programs menu.

Point to this option to open the Accessories menu.

Timely Tip

If you make a mistake as you are working on this exercise, you can issue the Undo command by choosing Undo from the Edit menu. This command allows you to erase any mistakes. The keyboard shortcut for this command is (CTRL) + Z.

Click to start the Paint program. If necessary, click the Maximize button to enlarge the Paint window. You should now see the application window shown in Figure 2.1. The tool box with its buttons appears on the left side of the window. You will now create the computer image shown in Figure 2.2.

FIGURE 2.1 The application window for the Paint program.

FIGURE 2.2 The computer image you will create in this exercise.

2. Create the outside of the monitor shown in Figure 2.3.

Click to activate the Rectangle tool.

Click and drag Click to anchor the upper-left corner of the monitor outline, and then drag down and to the right until the outline appears as shown in Figure 2.3.

3. Create the screen of the monitor shown in Figure 2.4.

Click to activate the Rounded Rectangle tool.

Click and drag Click to anchor the upper-left corner of the screen outline, and then drag down and to the right until the screen outline appears as shown in Figure 2.4.

FIGURE 2.3 The outline of the monitor created by using the Rectangle button.

FIGURE 2.4 The outline of the monitor screen created by using the Rounded Rectangle button.

4. Draw the brightness and contrast knobs on the monitor shown in Figure 2.5.

 Click to activate the Brush tool.

 Click on the first dot icon to activate this shape and size.

Click Click in the correct positions on the drawn monitor to draw the knobs shown in Figure 2.5.

FIGURE 2.5 **The brightness and contrast knobs added to the monitor.**

5. Create the stem of the monitor stand shown in Figure 2.6.

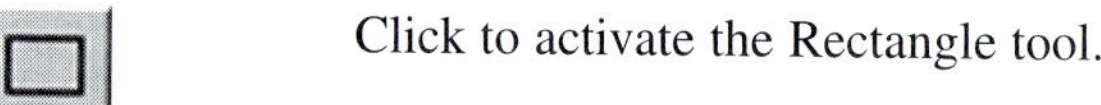

Click to activate the Rectangle tool.

Click and drag Click to anchor the upper-left corner of the monitor stand stem, and then drag down and to the right until the stem appears as shown in Figure 2.6.

6. Create the base of the monitor shown in Figure 2.7.

Click and drag Click to anchor the upper-left corner of the base outline, and then drag down and to the right until the base appears as shown in Figure 2.7.

FIGURE 2.6 **The stem of the monitor stand created by using the Rectangle button.**

FIGURE 2.7 The base of the monitor created by using the Rectangle button.

7. Create the system box beneath the monitor shown in Figure 2.8.

Click and drag Click to anchor the upper-left corner of the system box, and then drag down and to the right until the system box appears as shown in Figure 2.8.

8. Draw the air vent openings shown in Figure 2.9.

Click to activate the Line tool.

SHIFT, **Click and drag** Hold down the SHIFT key, click to anchor the top location of each vent, and then drag down to the ending location until the vertical vents appear as shown in Figure 2.9. Holding down the Shift key guarantees a straight line.

FIGURE 2.8 The outline of the system box created by using the Rectangle button.

FIGURE 2.9 The system box with the vertical vents added.

9. Add the 31/2-inch disk drive opening shown in Figure 2.10.

SHIFT, Click and drag Hold down the SHIFT key, click to anchor the left location of the drive opening, and then drag it to the ending location until the horizontal opening appears as shown in Figure 2.10.

FIGURE 2.10 The system box with the disk drive opening added.

10. Add the CD-ROM drive shown in Figure 2.11.

Click to activate the Rectangle feature.

Click and drag Click to anchor the upper-left corner of the CD-ROM drive outline, and then drag down and to the right until the drive outline appears as shown in Figure 2.11.

FIGURE 2.11 The CD-ROM drive added to the system box.

11. Color the system components light gray.

	Click this square of the color palette.
	Click to activate the Fill With Color tool.
Click	Click outside of the rounded rectangle screen to color the monitor frame.
Click	Click the stem of the monitor to color it.
Click	Click the base of the monitor to color it.
Click	Click the system box to color it. Your computer should now appear as shown in Figure 2.12.

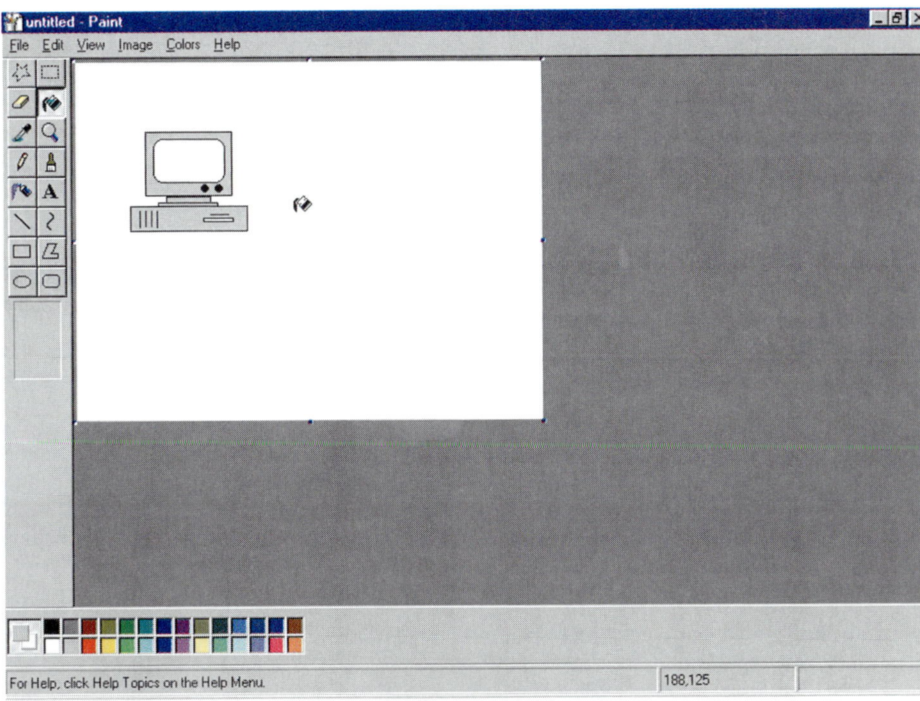

FIGURE 2.12 The system components colored gray.

12. Color the screen black.

Click on this square of the color palette (top row, first from the left).

Click Click inside the rounded rectangle screen to color the screen. Your finished computer should now appear as shown in Figure 2.13.

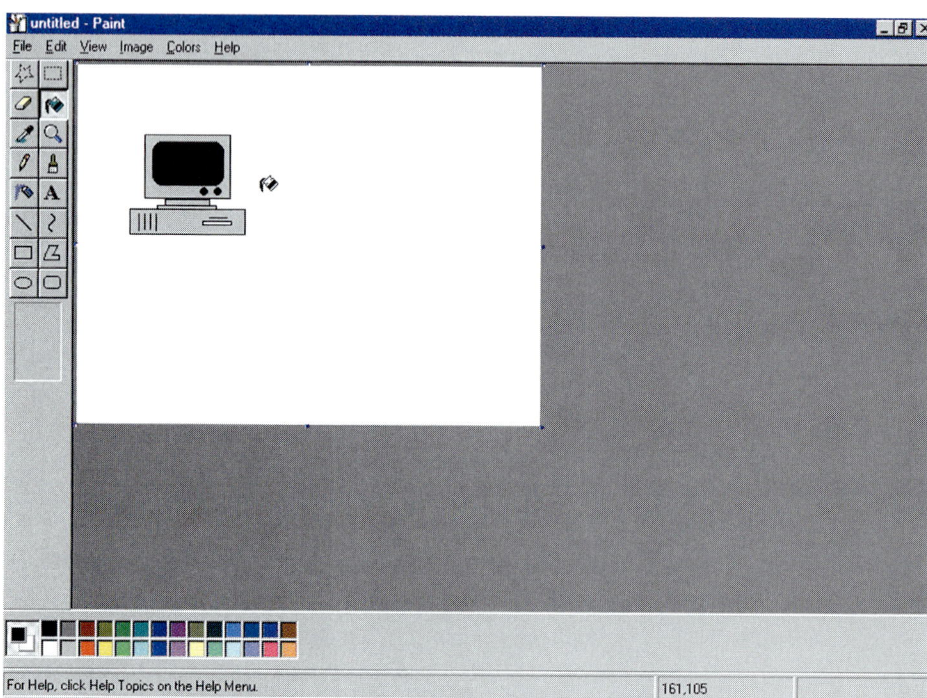

FIGURE 2.13 The finished computer with a black screen.

13. Copy the finished computer to the Windows clipboard.

Click to activate the Select feature.

Click and drag Place a selection rectangle around the finished computer. Your screen should now look like Figure 2.14.

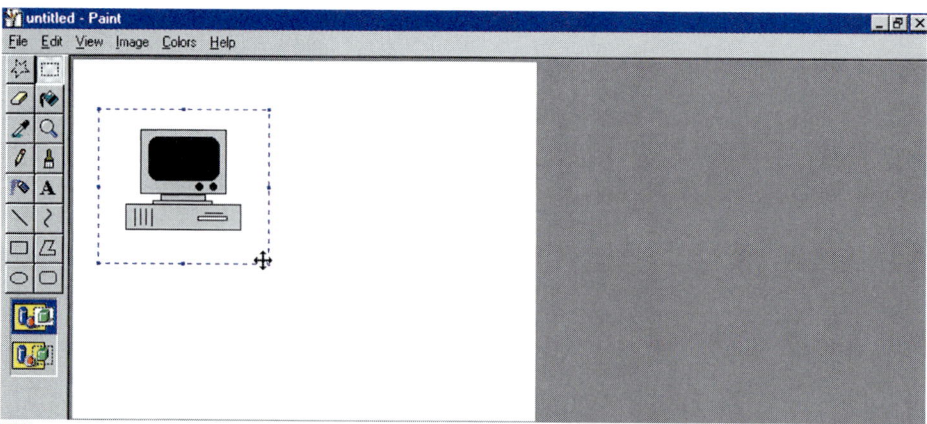

FIGURE 2.14 The selected computer drawing.

Edit	Select this option from the menu bar to open the Edit menu.
Copy	Select this option from the Edit menu to copy the contents of the selection to the Windows clipboard.

14. Paste a copy of the computer drawing.

Edit	Select this option from the menu bar to open the Edit menu.
Paste	Select this option to place a copy of the computer in the upper-left corner of the screen.
Click and drag	Move the copied computer drawing to the location shown in Figure 2.15 by dragging the selection.
Click	Click anywhere outside the drawing to cancel the selection.

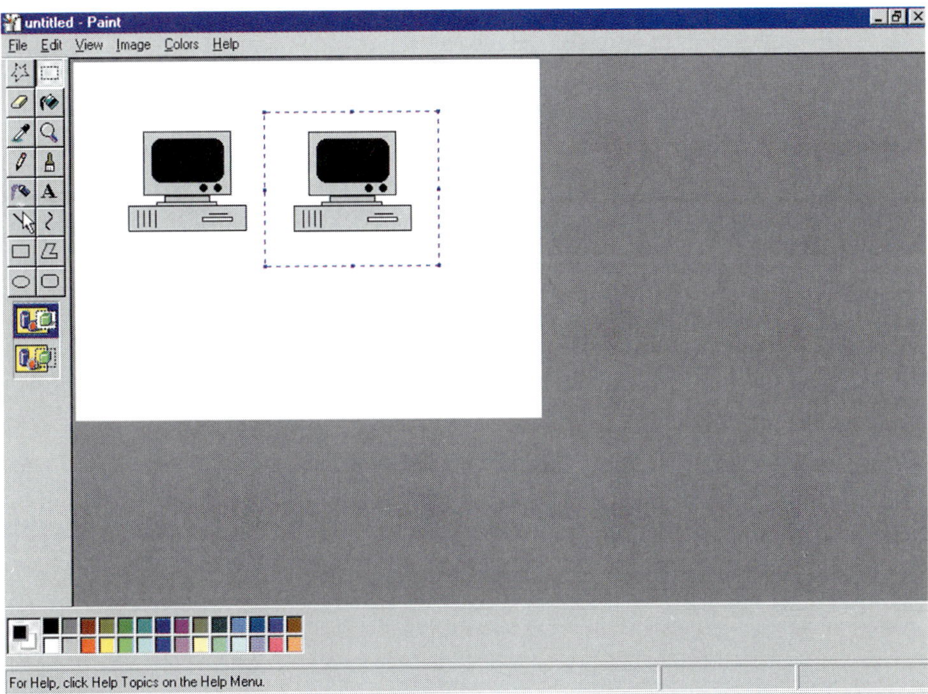

FIGURE 2.15 The copied computer placed next to the original computer drawing.

15. Use a keyboard shortcut command to paste an additional copy of the computer from the clipboard into the Paint window.

CTRL + **V**	Paste another copy of the computer in the upper-left corner of the screen.
Click and drag	Move the copied computer drawing to the location shown in Figure 2.16 by dragging the selection.

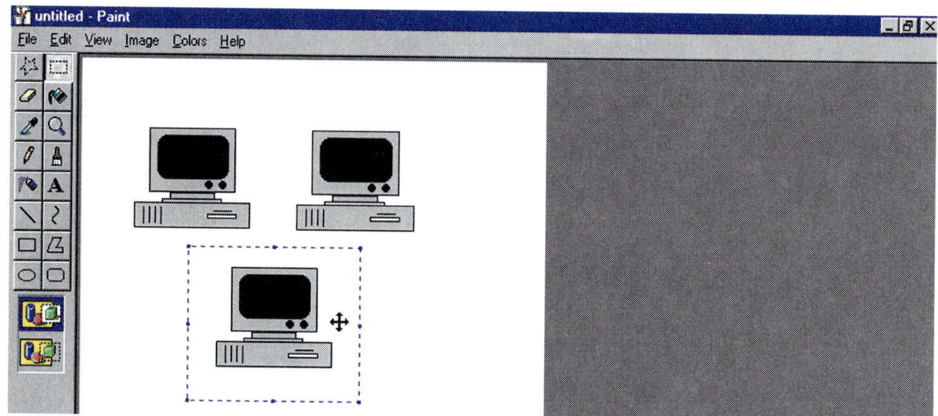

FIGURE 2.16 The third copy of the computer placed beneath the first two computers.

16. Print the drawing.

File	Click to open the File menu.
Print . . .	Click to open the Print dialog box shown in Figure 2.17.
OK	Print the drawing.

17. Save the picture to a diskette that you have placed in drive A.

File	Click to open the File menu.
Save As . . .	Click to open the Save As dialog box shown in Figure 2.18

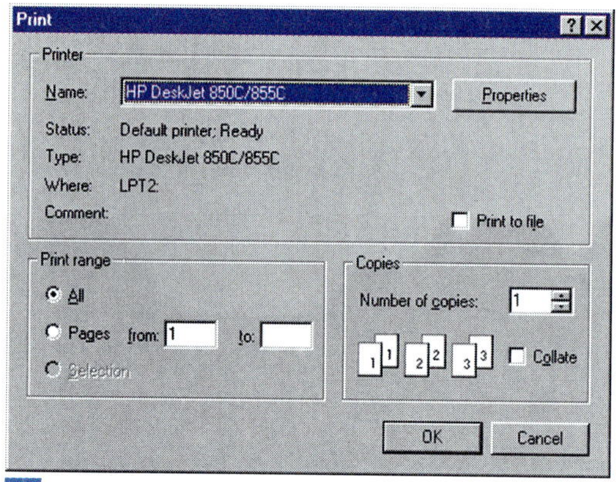

FIGURE 2.17 The Print dialog box of Paint.

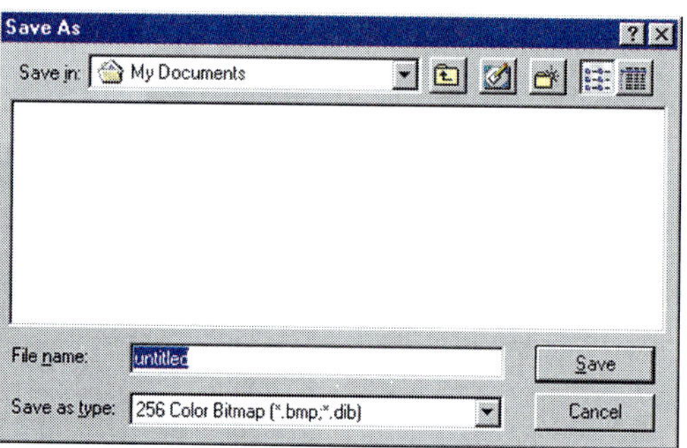

FIGURE 2.18 The Save As dialog box of Paint.

Type: `Computer`	Enter the name of the file.
Save in	Click the Save in selection box to get a listing of storage resources shown in Figure 2.19.
3½ Floppy (A:)	Click this entry. Your completed Save As dialog box should now look like Figure 2.20.
Save	Click the Save button to save the Computer picture to the diskette in drive A.

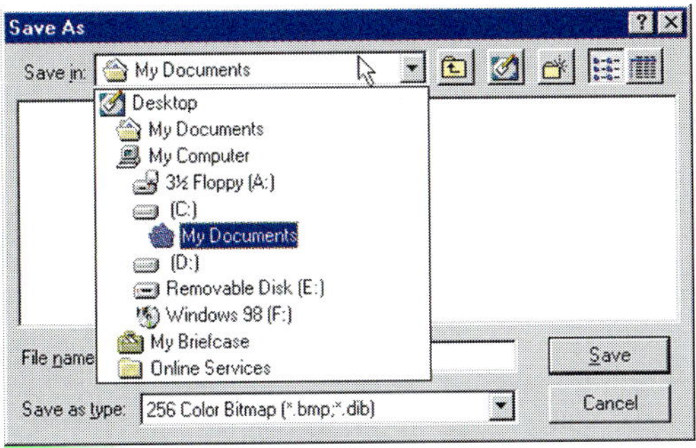

FIGURE 2.19 The available storage resources.

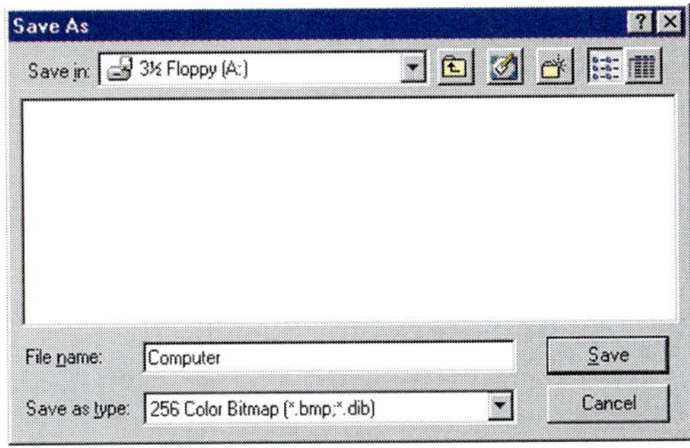

FIGURE 2.20 The completed Save As dialog box for saving the Paint computer picture.

18. Return to the desktop.

Click the Close button on the title bar.

Reinforcing the Exercise

1. Using the tools from the Paint tool box, you can draw and color a wide variety of images.
2. Before you can copy an object, you must select that object.
3. You use the Edit, Paste command sequence to place a copy of an object in a Paint window.
4. You can also use the (CTRL) + V keyboard shortcut to perform a Paste command.
5. The selected Paint button controls what type of object is being drawn.
6. Once a Paint button is selected a mouse operation is used to create the desired effect.
7. Holding down the (SHIFT) key while creating some line-based objects results in all straight lines.
8. You can save a picture to diskette.

VIEWING THE CLIPBOARD

Once you have copied information to the clipboard as we just did in the previous hands-on exercise, you can use the **Clipboard Viewer** of Windows to see just exactly what resides in the Clipboard. The Clipboard Viewer is accessed from the System Tools option of the Accessories menu. If you issue the command sequence Start, Programs, Accessories, System Tools, Clipboard Viewer, the contents of the Clipboard appear in the Clipboard Viewer like that shown in Figure 2.21.

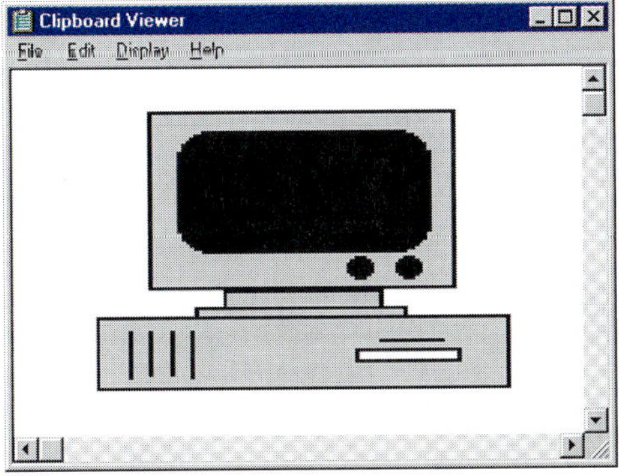

FIGURE 2.21 The computer image shown in the Clipboard Viewer window.

ACCESSING THE WINDOWS HELP FEATURE

The Windows **Help feature** provides several different types of help. You can access help by using ToolTips, the What's this button, the Help option of the Start menu, or ScreenTips.

USING TOOLTIPS

A ToolTip is a small text box that appears when you position the pointer on a control. It was introduced in the prior session.

TIMELY TIP

If you don't want to use the mouse, you can access help in most Windows applications or dialog boxes by pressing the F1 function key.

USING THE WHAT'S THIS BUTTON

The **What's this button** contains a question mark (?) and usually appears at the top of the open window or dialog box. If there is no What's this button displayed, look for a Help command button.

Once you click the What's this button, a question mark appears to the right of the pointer, indicating that you are in Help mode. When you click an item in the window or dialog box, a **ScreenTip** appears with a description about the control that you clicked.

TIMELY TIP

You can also many times activate a ScreenTip by right-clicking the object you need information about. A context menu appears, and you choose What's this? to display a ScreenTip. It should be noted that not all objects contain a What's this option in the displayed context menu.

USING THE START BUTTON

You access Windows' primary Help feature by choosing Help from the Start menu. Invoking the Help command in this way opens the Help Topics dialog box, which is composed of three tabs: Contents, Index, and Search. Use the **Contents tab** to locate information on general topics. Use the **Index tab** to locate information using keywords. Use the **Search tab** to search for text related to a topic of interest.

The Content tab in the Help feature of Windows makes use of Web links to access information. This means that as you position the mouse in the Help window it takes the shape of a hand with an extended index finger. As the mouse pointer is moved over a topic/link, the topic text becomes blue and underlined to indicate a link. A single click of the mouse then displays the information (Web page) for that link. Information found in the Index and Search tabs of the Help feature is located by double-clicking the desired topic.

Hands-On Exercise: Using the Windows Help Feature

1. Examine a ToolTip.

FIGURE 2.22 A ToolTip displayed for the clock icon of the Windows taskbar.

11:22 AM Point to the time in the status bar, and let the pointer stay there until a ToolTip with the day and date appears (Figure 2.22).

2. Examine a ScreenTip in a dialog box.

Double-click the My Computer icon to open that window.

View Click to open the View menu.

Folder Options . . . Click to open the Folder Options dialog box.

View Click to activate the View tab of the dialog box.

Reset All Folders Right-click the second command button in the dialog box, which has this text. A context menu with only the What's this? entry appears.

What's this? Click to display the ScreenTip for this entry (Figure 2.23).

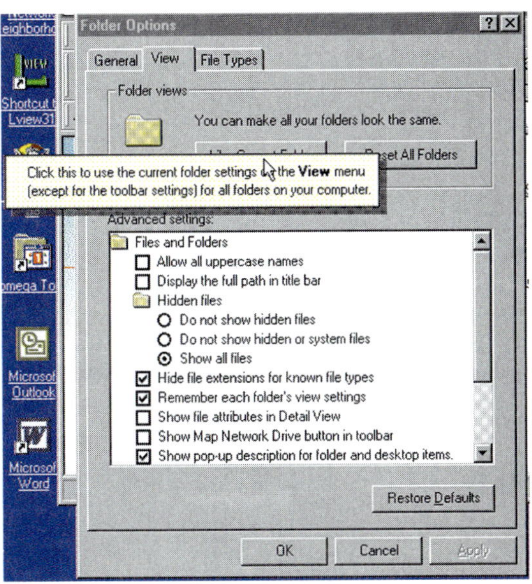

FIGURE 2.23 The ScreenTip for the second Reset All Folders button of the View tab of the Folder Options dialog box.

Click Click in any unused area of the window if necessary to close the ScreenTip.

Cancel Click Cancel to close the Folder Options dialog box.

X Click Close to close the My Computer window.

3. Open the Help dialog box.

Click to display the Start menu.

Help Click to display the Help Topics dialog box (Figure 2.24). The Contents tab should be displayed. If it isn't, click that tab to activate it. In the displayed list, each book icon represents a general topic that, when selected, will generate a new list of topics.

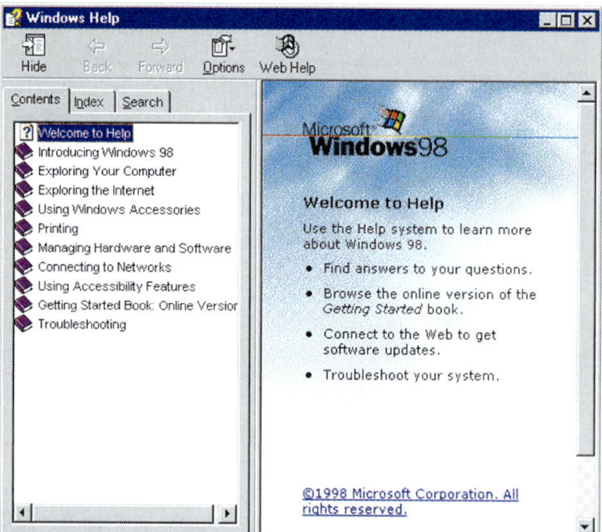

FIGURE 2.24 The Help Topics dialog box with three tabs.

4. Display a link.

Troubleshooting Point to this general topic to display the link for this entry (Figure 2.25).

5. Use the Contents tab to obtain help.

Using Windows Accessories Click this topic. The book icon changes to an open book, and a number of topics appear beneath it (Figure 2.26).

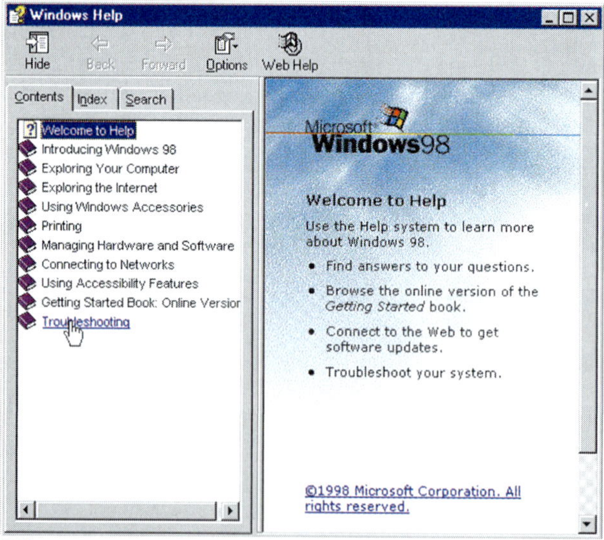

FIGURE 2.25 The link generated when you position to the Troubleshooting entry.

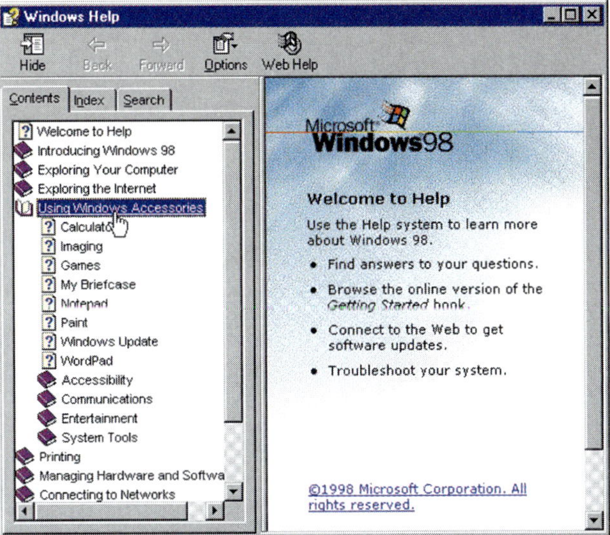

FIGURE 2.26 The topics displayed by selecting the Using Windows Accessories topic.

System Tools Click this topic to generate another list of topics (Figure 2.27). Selecting a question mark icon generates a Help screen.

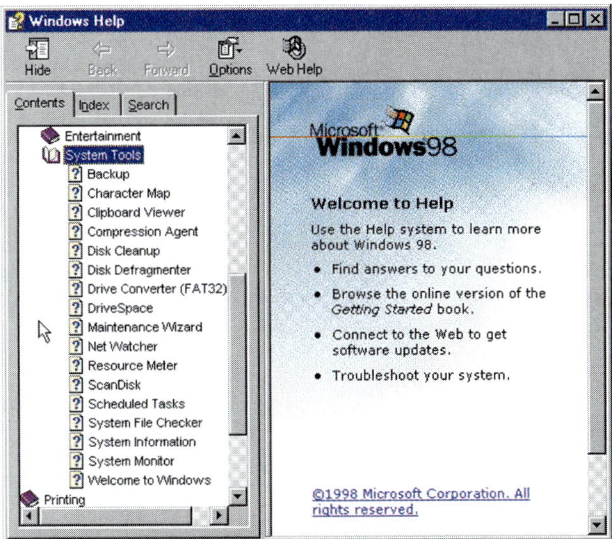

FIGURE 2.27 The topics displayed by selecting the System Tools Help topic.

Clipboard Viewer Click this topic to generate the Help screen shown in Figure 2.28.

Options Click to display the Options menu.

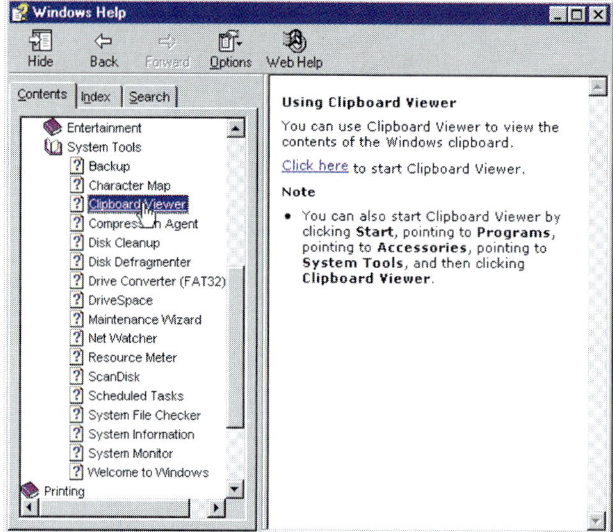

FIGURE 2.28 The Clipboard Viewer Help screen.

TIMELY TIP

Clicking a document with a question mark displays a help document for the indicated topic in the right-hand pane of the Help window.

Print . . . Click to open the Print dialog box (Figure 2.29).

OK Click to print the text only from the current page of the Help window and display the second Print dialog box shown in Figure 2.30.

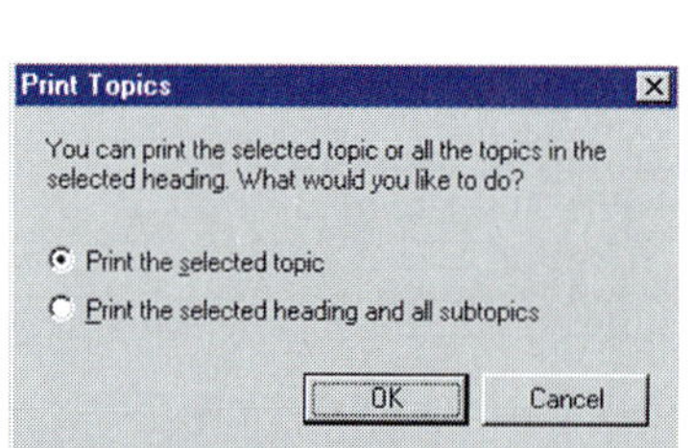

FIGURE 2.29 The Print dialog box for determining what is to be printed.

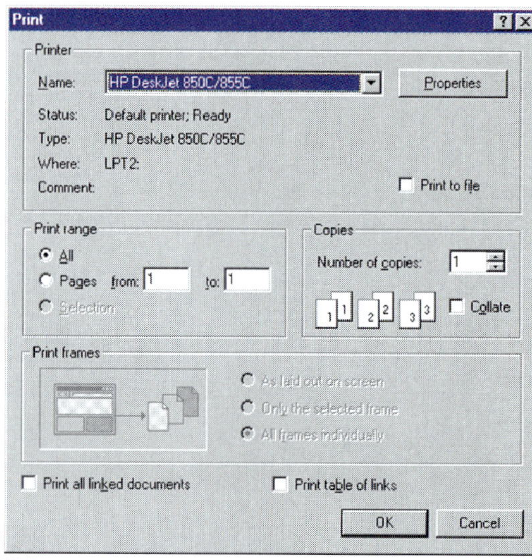

FIGURE 2.30 The Print dialog box.

OK Click to print the text.

6. Close the open topics.

System Tools Slowly click this option to close this book of topics.

Using Windows Accessories Slowly click this option to close this book of topics and general topics. Topics displayed in the left-hand box should now look like Figure 2.24.

7. Get information about keyboard shortcuts. Note that the help information in the right-hand pane of the Help window does not change as you move from one topic to the next.

Exploring Your Computer Click on this link to get a listing of general topics (Figure 2.31).

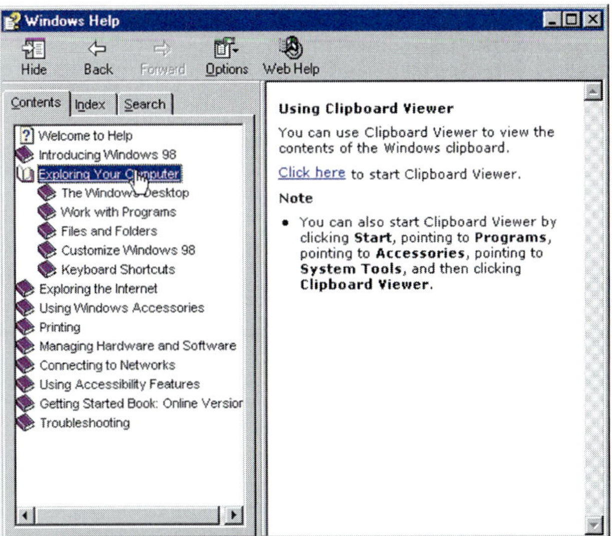

FIGURE 2.31 The topics for the Exploring Your Computer link.

Keyboard Shortcuts Click on this link to get a list of topics (Figure 2.32).

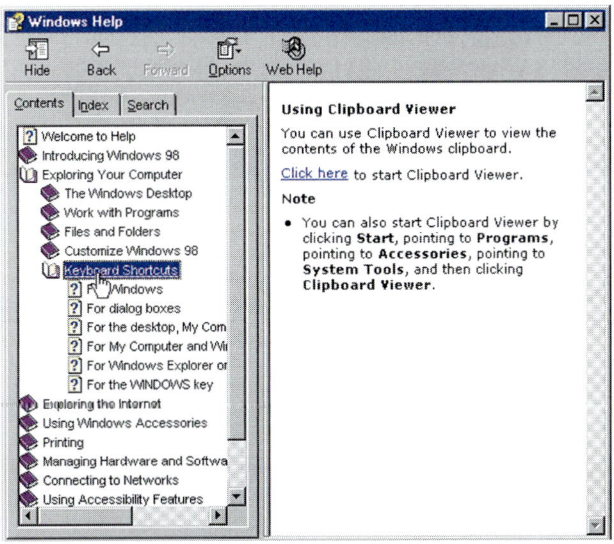

FIGURE 2.32 The topics for the Keyboard Shortcuts link.

For Windows Click this link to get the Help document information like that shown in Figure 2.33.

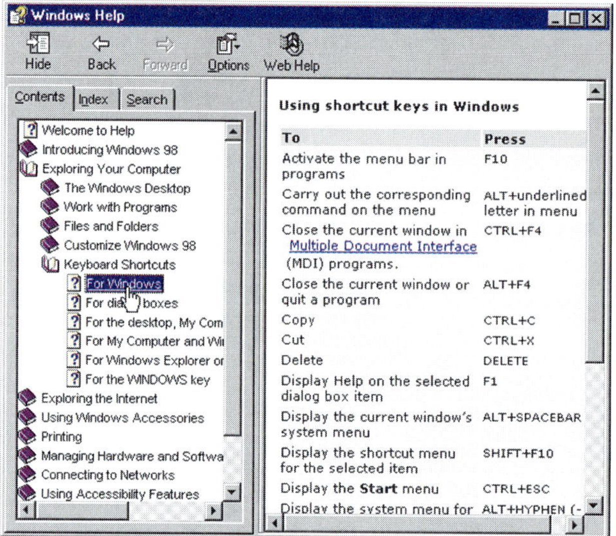

FIGURE 2.33 The Help information for shortcut keys in Windows.

8. Print the help information.

Options	Click to display the Options menu.
Print . . .	Click to open the Print dialog box that determines what you want printed.
OK	Click to print the text only from the current page of the Help window and display the second Print dialog box.
 OK	Click to print the text. You might want to save this page for future reference.

9. Access help for printing documents using the Index tab. Note, the right-hand pane remains the same.

Index	Activate the Index tab (Figure 2.34).

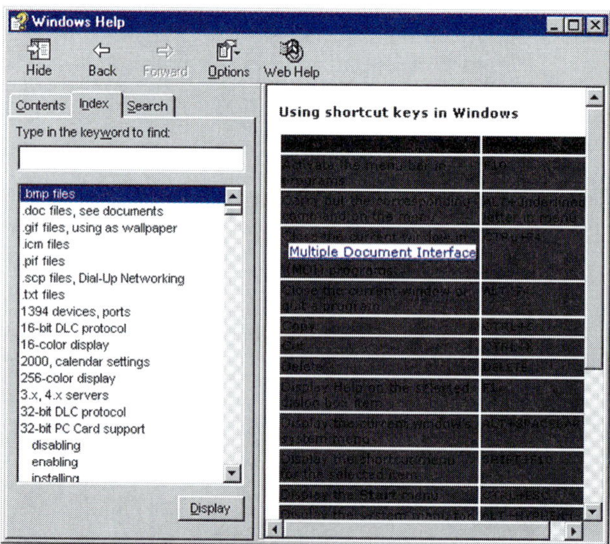

FIGURE 2.34 The Index tab provides a search feature that locates the topic you want.

Type: `printing` Enter this text in the text box at the top of the Index tab. A list of related topics appears in the lower list box (Figure 2.35).

Documents Double-click this topic to display the Help screen shown in Figure 2.36.

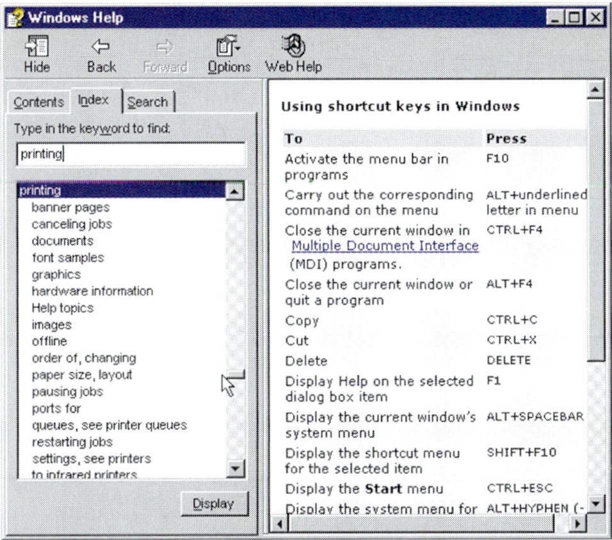

FIGURE 2.35 The matching Help topics located for the printing topic.

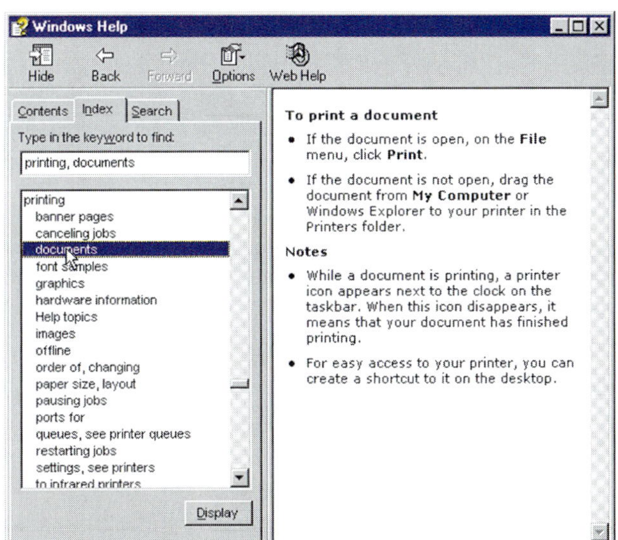

FIGURE 2.36 The Help screen for the printing documents topic.

10. Select and copy the text in the right-hand box.

Click and drag Use a drag operation to select all of the text in the right-hand box. It should now appear in a different color.

CTRL **+ C** Use the Copy keyboard shortcut to copy the text to the clipboard.

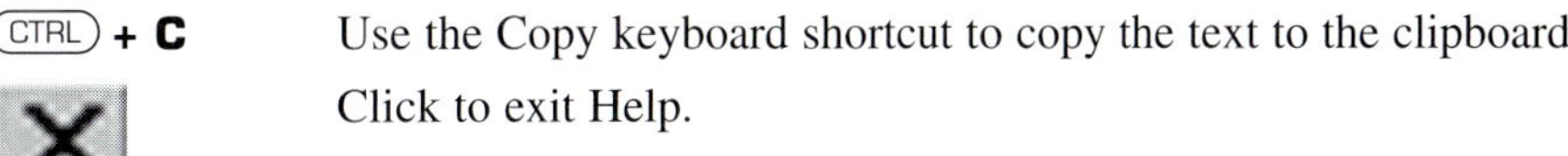

Click to exit Help.

11. WordPad is Window's built-in word processor. Open the WordPad program, and look at the text you copied to the clipboard.

Click to open the Start menu.

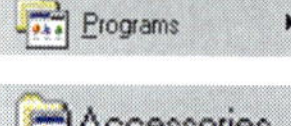

Open the Programs menu.

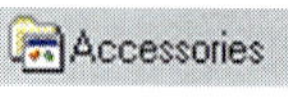

Open the Accessories menu.

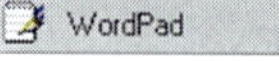

Click to start WordPad. The window shown in Figure 2.37 appears.

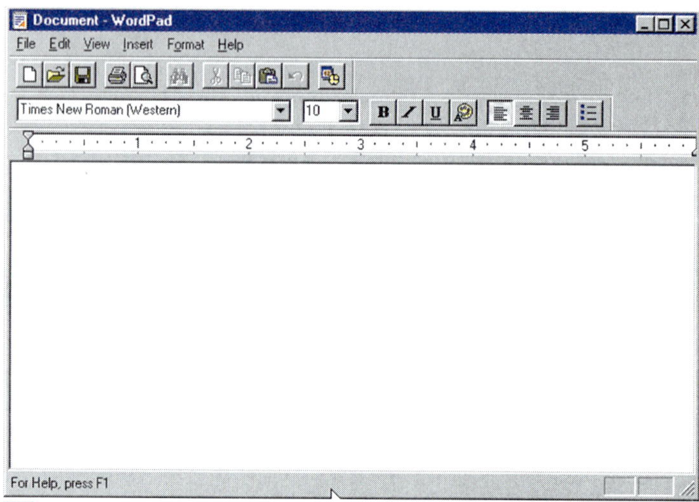

FIGURE 2.37 The WordPad application window.

Edit Open the Edit pull-down menu.

Paste Click to copy the text from the clipboard. The WordPad window should now look like Figure 2.38. The text appears on-screen exactly as it will print to paper. This is referred to as "what you see is what you get" or **WYSIWYG**.

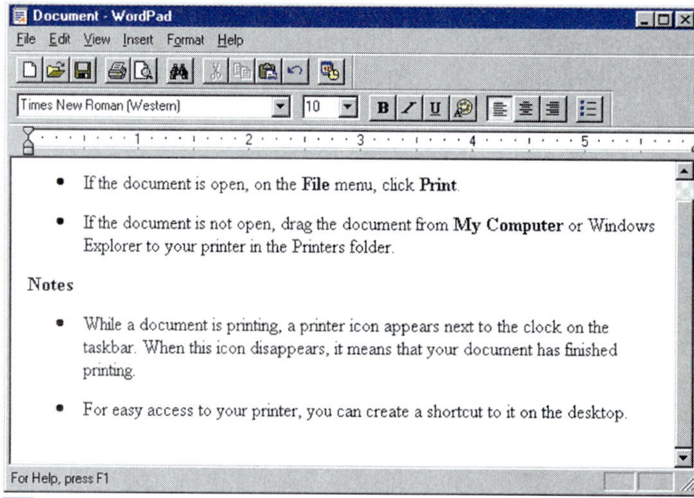

FIGURE 2.38 The text from the clipboard as it appears in the WordPad window.

Click to print the document. Your printed page should look exactly like the document on-screen.

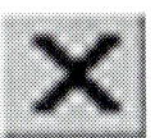

Click to return to the Windows desktop. WordPad now displays a dialog box that asks if you want to save changes to the document (Figure 2.39).

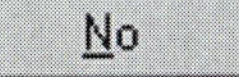

Click to return to the desktop without saving changes.

12. Issue the command sequence Start, Programs, Accessories, System Tools, Clipboard Viewer, to see the contents of the Clipboard. The Clipboard Viewer should appear like that shown in Figure 2.40.

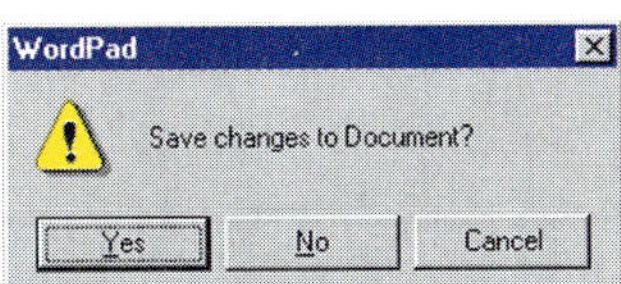

FIGURE 2.39 The WordPad dialog box prompting you about saving any changes.

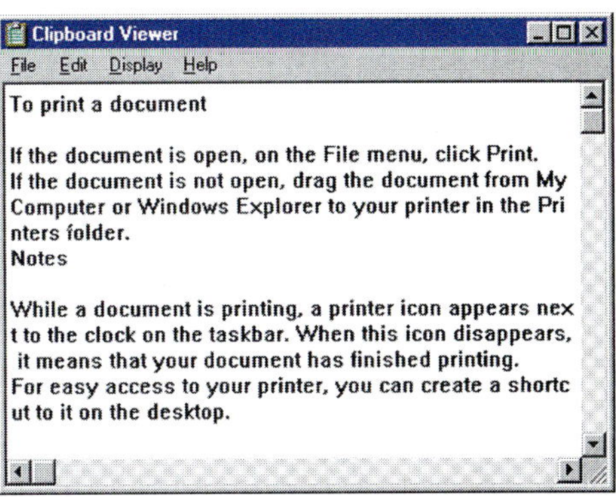

FIGURE 2.40 The Clipboard Viewer window with the Printing a Document information copied previously.

Reinforcing the Exercise

1. When you point to an object and allow the pointer to remain on the object for a short time, a ToolTip appears, displaying information about that object.
2. When you click the What's this button, a question mark appears on the right side of the pointer.
3. You can open a ScreenTip by right-clicking the object you need information on and then choosing What's this? from the context menu.
4. The Help Topics dialog box has three tabs: Contents, Index, and Search.
5. Items on the Contents tab of the Help box appear as links.
6. Help documents from the Index and Search tabs are accessed using a double-click of the mouse.
7. Information can be copied to the clipboard from a help box and accessed later.

On Your Own

You may have heard that Windows 98 has the ability to do such things as play multimedia files that you have downloaded from a Web site or to use the Web to access additional help information. To find out more about these topics, access the Windows Help feature. Once the Help feature is displayed do the following.

- To access the online Help feature, click the Web Help button on the Standard toolbar of the Help window. Once you click the Support Online link, you will be connected to the Microsoft Web site from which you can get access to more help information.
- To find out more information about the multimedia capabilities of Windows 98, activate either the Index or Search tabs and enter the term *multimedia* as the item for which you wish to perform the search. Examine any of the entries that strike your fancy. Figure 2.41 shows some of the topics that appear in the Search tab for the term *multimedia*.

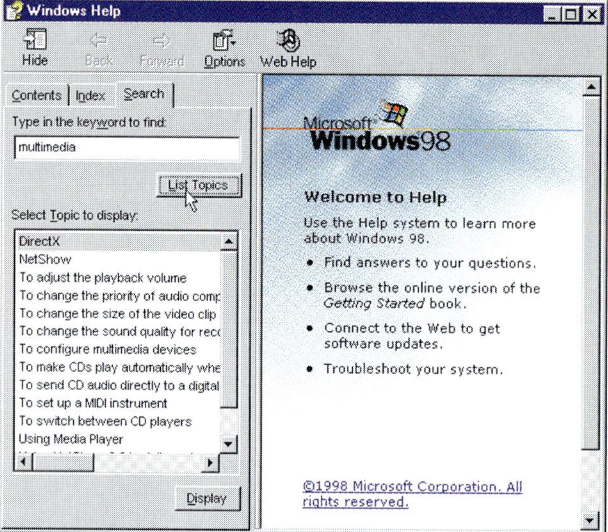

FIGURE 2.41 **The Help window with information about the multimedia topic in the Search tab.**

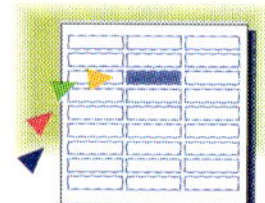

On Your Own

You may have access to a computer that you have to share with a number of other people. For instance, you might be sharing a computer in an apartment, a dorm room, or with other family members. In such a situation, people may have different ideas about which Windows features they want to have activated. Some may like the Web features of Windows 98 while others may not. Windows allows you to personalize Windows to each user using the Password feature. To customize Windows on your computer so that it can be used by others do the following:

- Access the Help feature of Windows and invoke the Search tab.
- Perform a search using the words *multiple users*.
- Follow the instructions given in the Help feature for invoking this feature.

Session Review

Windows uses a temporary storage area called the clipboard to hold information that was used in a Copy or Cut command. The clipboard can only hold information from one command. If you execute another Cut or Copy the prior contents are replaced with the results from the new command. A Paste command copies information from the clipboard to the insertion point location. The Cut, Copy, and Paste commands can be executed using menu sequences or keyboard shortcut commands.

The Paint program is found in the Accessories menu. Using Paint, you can exercise your artistic talents to draw a picture by invoking one of the drawing tools and then manipulating that tool using mouse operations. Once a picture has been created, you can create multiple copies of that picture by using the Copy and Paste commands.

You can access the Help feature of Windows by choosing Help from the Start menu or by using ToolTips, ScreenTips, or the What's this button. You can also copy information from Help screens into the Windows clipboard and print the information. The general topics of the Contents tab in the Windows Help window are Web links. Information from these links can be accessed via a single click. Topics from the Index and Search tabs are accessed using a double-click.

Key Terms and Concepts

Session Quiz

Multiple Choice

1. Which of the following commands places information on the clipboard?
   - **a.** Copy
   - **b.** Insert
   - **c.** Paste
   - **d.** Clipboard Viewer
2. Which command destroys current data on the clipboard?
   - **a.** Copy
   - **b.** Insert
   - **c.** Paste
   - **d.** Clipboard Viewer
3. Holding down the ____________ key allows you to draw straight lines using a number of Paint features.
   - **a.** CTRL
   - **b.** INS
   - **c.** ALT
   - **d.** SHIFT
4. The ____________ tab of the Help window contains Web-like links to help topics and information.
   - **a.** Web
   - **b.** Index
   - **c.** Link
   - **d.** Contents
5. Which of the following statement(s) about the Help feature is (are) true?
   - **a.** You can sometimes activate the Help feature by pressing the F1 key.
   - **b.** Clicking the What's this button changes the appearance of the pointer.
   - **c.** The Help feature allows you to copy text from Help screens to the clipboard.
   - **d.** You cannot look up information about a specific topic using the Help feature.

True/False

6. The clipboard holds information that has been placed in it using a Cut or Paste command.
7. The Paint program requires you to make use of the mouse in drawing various objects.
8. Information is deleted from the clipboard each time a Paste command is executed.
9. Help information that resides in the right-hand pane of the Help window changes automatically as you move from one general topic to another in the left-hand window.
10. The keyboard shortcut command for the Paste command is CTRL + P.

Session Review Exercises

1. Define or describe each of the following:
   - **a.** ScreenTip
   - **b.** Clipboard Viewer
   - **c.** Paint program
   - **d.** Web link
   - **e.** clipboard
2. The ____________ acts as a temporary storage area and allows you to copy text or graphics to it.
3. The ____________ or ____________ commands place information in the clipboard.
4. The ____________ or ____________ commands replace the current contents of the clipboard.

5. The ____________ command copies the clipboard contents to the insertion point.
6. The ____________, ____________ menu command sequence is used to place clipboard information at the insertion point location.
7. The ____________ + ____________ keyboard shortcut command is used to execute a Copy command.
8. The ____________ ____________ can be used to display the contents of the clipboard.
9. The Clipboard Viewer is found in the ____________ of the Accessories menu.
10. The ____________ program is found in the Accessories menu and is used to create freehand drawings.
11. Buttons found in the Paint ____________ ____________ control what objects or affects can be applied to the drawing in the Paint window.
12. The ____________ ____________ is used to control the color of an object in the Paint window.
13. Holding down the ____________ key results in a straight line when using a number of paint commands that use lines.
14. The Help window is activated using the Windows ____________ button.
15. The ____________ tab of the Help window contains Web links.
16. A ____________ is activated using the What's this option of a context menu.
17. The ____________ tab of the Help window is used to locate information on general topics.
18. The ____________ tab of the Help window is used to locate information using keywords.
19. Pressing the ____________ key activates the Help feature of Windows when you are in an application program.
20. A help document appears in the ____________-hand pane of the Help window.

Computer Exercises

1. Activate the Help widow from the Start button. If you are new to the Windows environment do the following:
   - a. Click the Getting Started Book: Online Version link.
   - b. Click the Microsoft Windows 98 Getting Started link.
   - c. Click the Getting Started link in the right-hand pane. A new window now appears.
   - d. Examine the Using Your Desktop topic.
   - e. Print the Overview topic.
   - f. Examine the various topics that interest you.
   - g. Print out any topics that interest you.
2. Activate the Index tab.
   - a. Type in the topic *Address*.
   - b. Locate the Address Bar topic in the left-hand pane.
   - c. Double-click the toolbar overview topic.
   - d. Using the Options menu, print this help page.
   - e. Copy the Help information to the clipboard. Open a WordPad document and paste the information from the clipboard. Print the document. How do the two printouts differ?
   - f. View the clipboard contents using the Clipboard Viewer.
3. Activate the Search tab.
   - a. Enter the search topic of dragging.
   - b. Double-click a topic to get the help information displayed in the right-hand pane.
   - c. Print the Help page.
   - d. Close the Help window.
4. Practice using other Windows Help features.
   - a. Double-click the time in the taskbar to open the Date/Time Properties dialog box.
   - b. Right-click the clock, and then click the What's this? menu entry. A ScreenTip now appears. Click anywhere to make the text box disappear.
   - c. Click on the calendar portion of the dialog box. Press the F1 key and a Help text box appears for the calendar. Click anywhere to make the text box disappear.
   - d. Click the What's this icon at the top of the Date/Time Properties dialog box. A question mark now appears beside the pointer. Click the OK button at the bottom of the dialog box. A Help text box appears. Click the Cancel button to close the Date/Time Properties dialog box.
5. Practice using the Paint program.

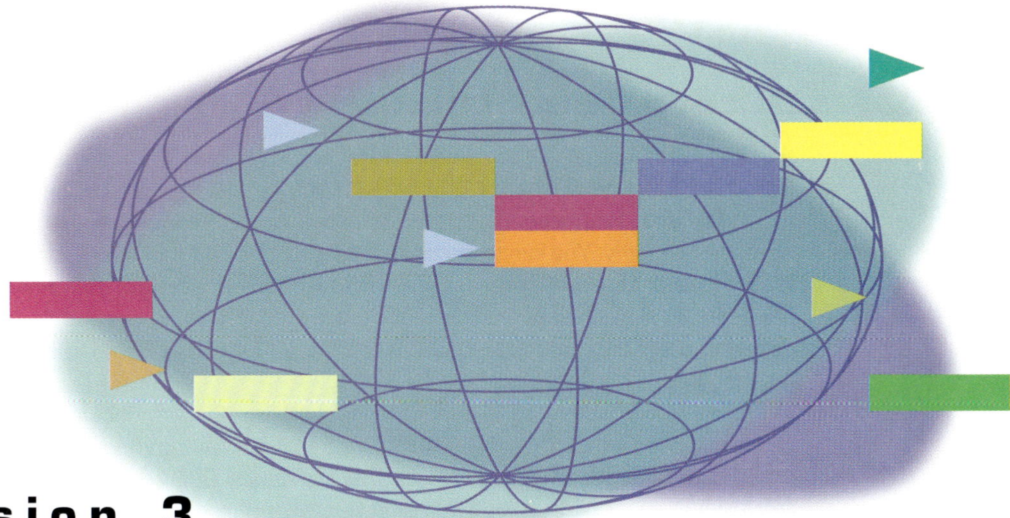

Session 3

Manipulating Documents and Folders

After completing this session, you should be able to:

- Distinguish between folders and documents
- Select multiple documents and folders
- Name, rename, delete, and copy documents and folders
- Create a folder
- Print a document
- Use the Print Manager
- Format a disk
- Use Windows Explorer

STORAGE OBJECTS

Windows provides many different commands that allow you to interact with objects that you have saved to disk. This process of interaction is called **file maintenance**. To make its file maintenance system easy to understand, Windows uses a **folder** metaphor, which refers to the standard manila folder that holds one or more documents for storage in a filing cabinet.

In Windows' metaphorical folder, each piece of paper, or **document**, represents stored data that can be processed by an application program or by the computer itself. The folder is in a unique location on a disk. A disk can contain many different folders, and a folder can contain other folders as well as documents. Folders can hold such things as parts of the operating system, word processing documents, workbooks for use by a spreadsheet, databases, and so forth.

A document is similar to a file but **file** is a computer term rather than a windows-related term. Windows generally uses the term *document*.

Folders and Documents

A folder is represented by a manila folder icon whenever you have information about a disk drive displayed on-screen (Figure 3.1). You can display the contents of a drive, with its folders and documents (files), by double-clicking the icon for that drive in the My Computer window. You can then open a folder by clicking it in Web view or double-clicking it in standard windows mode. Windows also provides control over how the icons in a folder are displayed in a window using View menu options. Figure 3.1 shows information displayed using the Large Icons view, while Figure 3.2 shows information displayed using the List view.

Once a folder is open in Classic Style, any other folders or documents that it contains are displayed in another window—this means that you get multiple open windows as you drill-down in the file system if you use My Computer (Figure 3.3). A document appears as a sheet of paper with an icon that indicates what type of information is stored in it. For instance, a Word document is represented by a sheet of paper with a big *W* toward the top of the page. A workbook file that was created by Excel appears with a large *X*. If Windows does not know what type of application program was used to create the document, it displays the Microsoft flag as the icon for that folder.

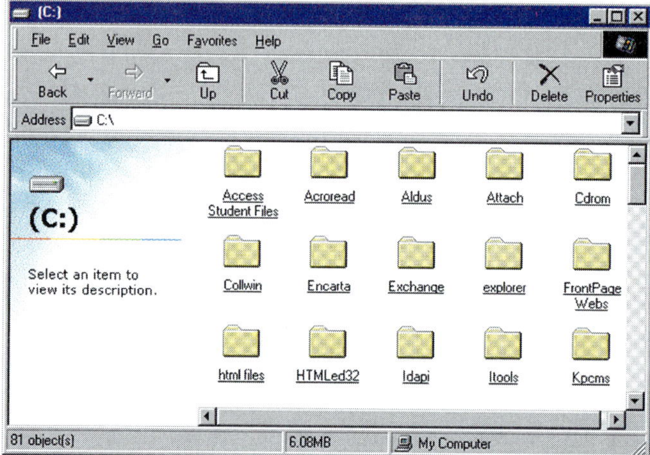

FIGURE 3.1 The drive C window with several folders visible. Your window may look dramatically different from this. For instance, you may have different software folders visible on your screen.

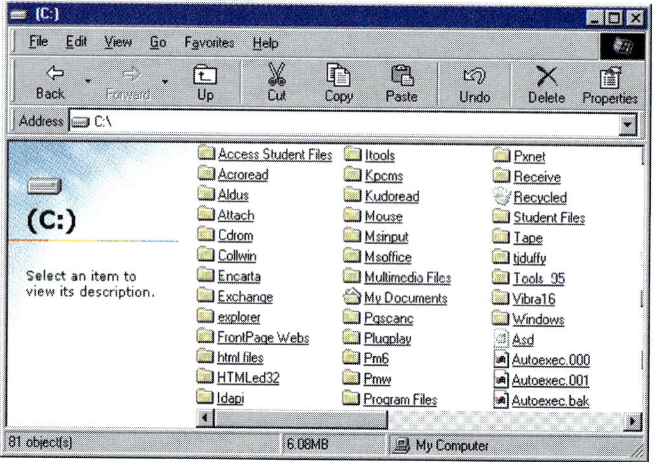

FIGURE 3.2 The same information displayed in Figure 3.1 shown using the List option of the View menu in Web Style.

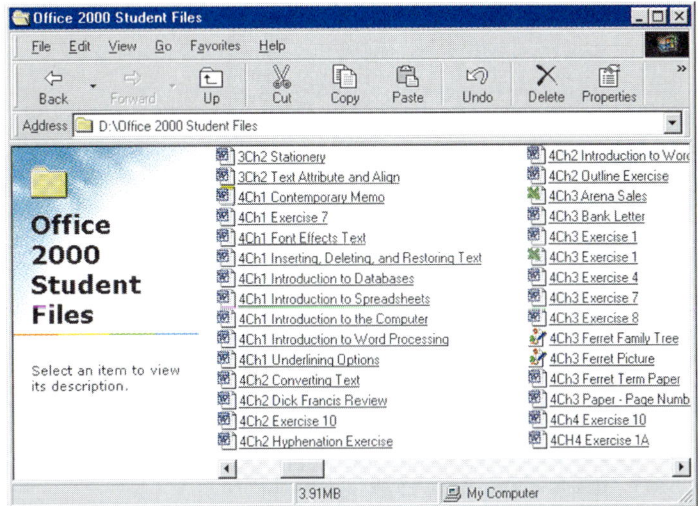

FIGURE 3.3 **The Office 2000 Student Files folder opened with several different types of files displayed. This folder was created for storing files related to this textbook.**

Naming a Folder or Document

When you name a folder or document, you want to generate a label that makes it easier to remember what's inside that folder or document. With Windows, you can use up to 255 characters, including spaces, in a folder or document name. This ability allows you to develop descriptive names more easily than you could with older versions of Windows or DOS.

Associating Documents with Applications

In a window like the one shown in Figure 3.3, a document with an application's logo as part of its icon is referred to as an associated document. An **associated document** has been created by a specific software application and, when the application was installed, the operating system was told how to recognize these documents. If you double-click the icon for an associated document, the software application that was used to create that document is started and the document is loaded.

If you try to open a document that Windows has not associated with an application, Windows displays an Open With dialog box like that shown in Figure 3.4. You must then scroll through the list box and double-click the application program that is to be used with the selected document.

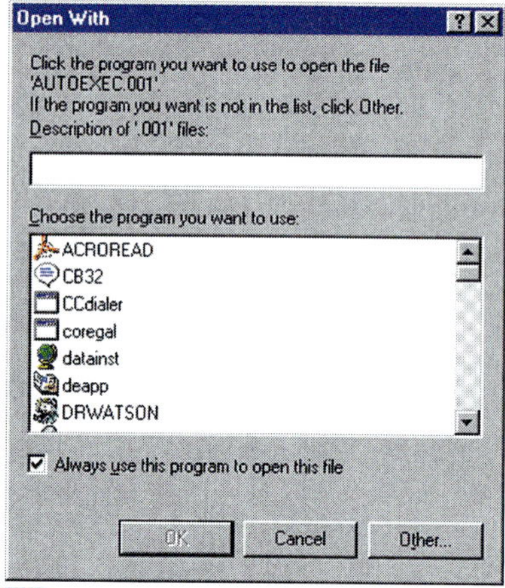

FIGURE 3.4 The Open With dialog box that appears when Windows does not know what application has been associated with a document.

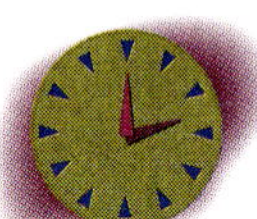

Timely Tip

As you explore the various features of Windows, you may be working directly with documents. In such a situation, Windows may temporarily truncate long document names and end them with a tilde (~). This convention allows Windows 98 to retain compatibility with older versions of Windows and DOS. When you return to the desktop of Windows, the longer names will be displayed.

Selecting Documents and Folders

To select a document, folder, or multiple documents or folders, you use the mouse. Remember that folders and documents can both be referred to as objects.

Selecting a Single Object

Web Mode: When you are using Web mode you select a single object by pointing to the object.

Classic Windows Mode: When you are using Classic Windows mode to select a single object that you want to work with, you click the icon that represents that object.

Once selected, the color of the document or folder icon changes to blue (or some other color). Once you have selected the correct object, you can issue a command and begin working with it.

Selecting Adjacent Objects

You can **select adjacent objects** (documents or folders) in one of two ways: using SHIFT or using a drag operation. To use SHIFT, you select the first object (using one of the above methods), hold down SHIFT, and then select the last object. All objects between the two selected objects are included in the selection and appear in blue.

To select multiple objects by using a drag operation, position the pointer to the left of the first object (if the object is in the first column of the window, position the mouse immediately to the right of it), and then click and drag to include the last object. As you drag the pointer, a rectangle forms around the objects, and the objects turn blue (Figure 3.5). When the selection includes all the objects you want to select, release the left mouse button. The rectangle disappears, but the objects remain blue to indicate that they are selected. If you find that you have included the wrong objects in the selection, you can cancel that selection by clicking any unused area of the window. Once you have the desired objects in the selection, you can issue a command.

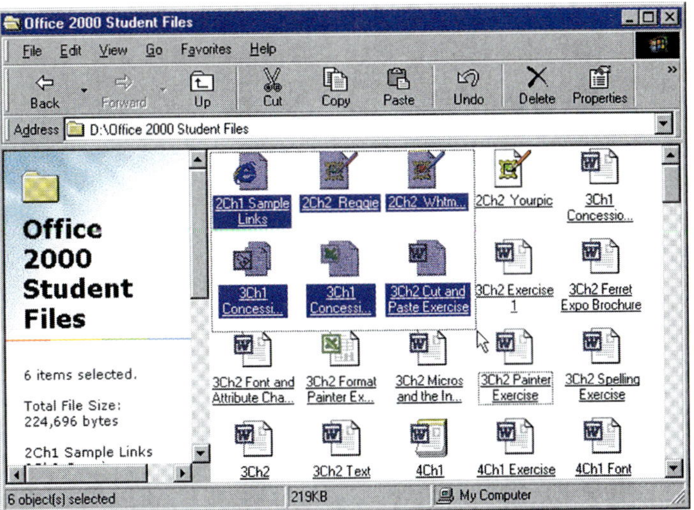

FIGURE 3.5 When you are using a drag operation to select multiple objects, a rectangle appears and the selected objects included in the selection appear in blue.

Timely Tip

Make certain that you do not begin a drag operation by positioning the pointer directly on the document or folder icon and clicking. If you do, you will be moving the object instead of including it in a selection. When such a mistake happens, just move the icon back to its original location. You can then click to the left of the icon to include it in the selection and complete the drag operation.

Selecting Nonadjacent Objects

To **select nonadjacent objects**, you hold down (CTRL) as you select the icons of the documents and folders that you want to operate on.

Timely Tip

If you inadvertently drag the pointer as you are holding down (CTRL), you will be executing a Copy command. After the Copy command is executed, one or more icons will appear on the screen labeled Copy of Document, with Document as the name of the document or folder that you inadvertently copied. To get rid of this, click the offending icon and press (DEL). A Confirm File Delete dialog box appears (Figure 3.6). Click the Yes button.

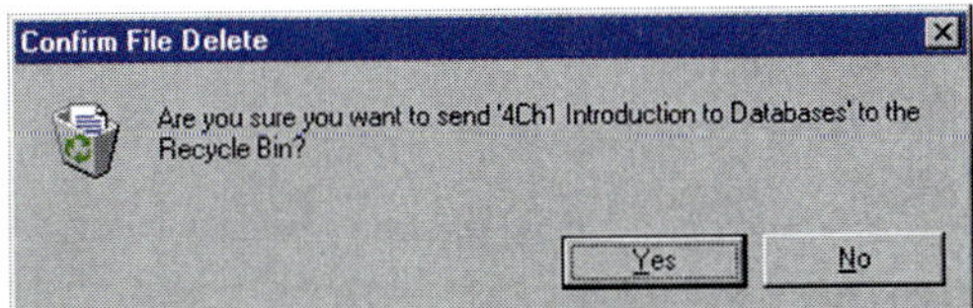

FIGURE 3.6 The Confirm File Delete dialog box.

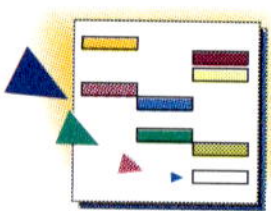

Hands-On Exercise: Manipulating Disk Objects

This hands-on exercise makes use of the documents that are used with this text. If your documents reside on a disk in drive A, follow the steps indicated in Step 1; otherwise, use the steps indicated by your instructor to get to the location of the documents to be used with this text. If your files do not reside on drive A, make certain that you write down the procedure to access those files so you will have it for future use.

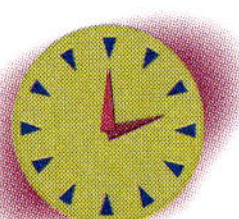

Timely Tip

How you select items in the following Hands-On exercise is dependent upon the interface that you have activated. If you are using the Web interface, a single click is all that is necessary to start a program or open an object. Pointing selects an item.

If you are using the Classic Windows interface, a double-click starts or opens an object, while a click selects an object.

1. Access the textbook documents.

Click to open the My Computer window. Make certain you have Web Style activated.

Open the 3 1/2 Floppy (A:) window or wherever your student data files for this textbook reside. A window listing the documents to be used with the text should now appear (Figure 3.7). If your window does not appear like Figure 3.7, issue the View, List commands.

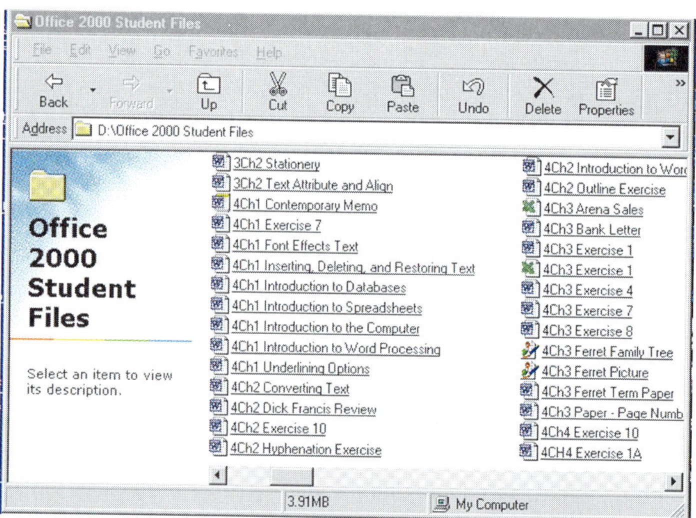

FIGURE 3.7 The window showing the textbook documents found on drive A or some other location.

2. Maximize the window.

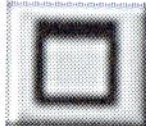

Click to maximize the window.

3. Select an associated document.

4Ch3 Ferret Family Tree Point to this file to select it. Your Student Files window (drive A for you) should now look like Figure 3.8. For some types of files, Windows provides this method of previewing the file contents.

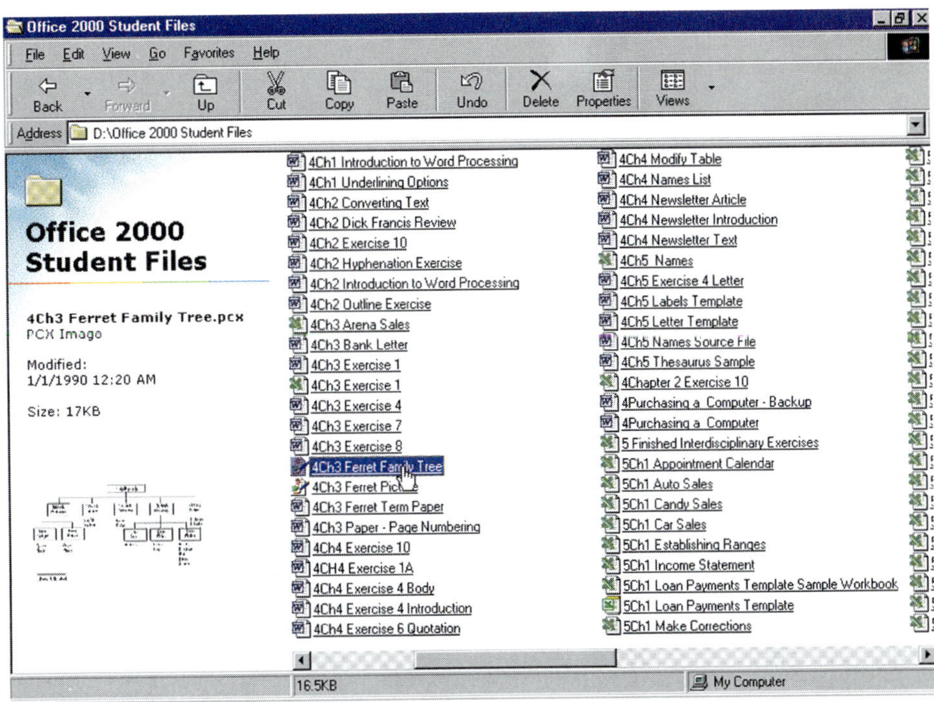

FIGURE 3.8 **The previewed 4Ch3 Ferret Family Tree document.**

4. Open an Excel associated document.

4Ch3 Exercise 1 Click this Excel workbook to start Excel and load this document. You should now see the Excel screen shown in Figure 3.9.

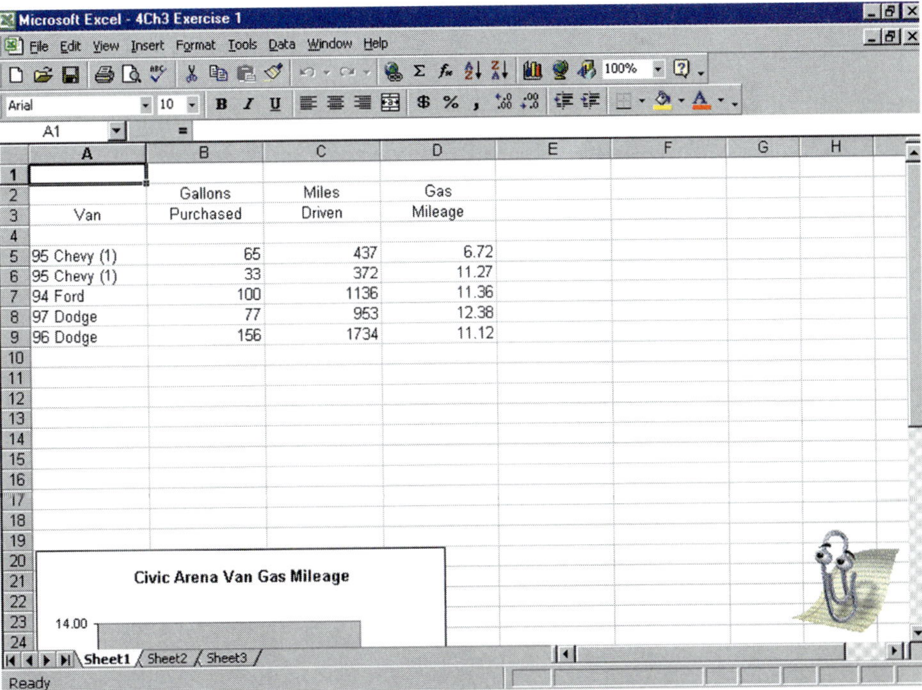

FIGURE 3.9 **The associated 4Ch3 Exercise 1 document displayed using Excel.**

Click the Close button on the Excel title bar to return to the window containing the textbook files.

5. Open a Word associated document.

4Ch1 Introduction to Word Processing Click to start Word and load this document. You should now see the Word screen shown in Figure 3.10.

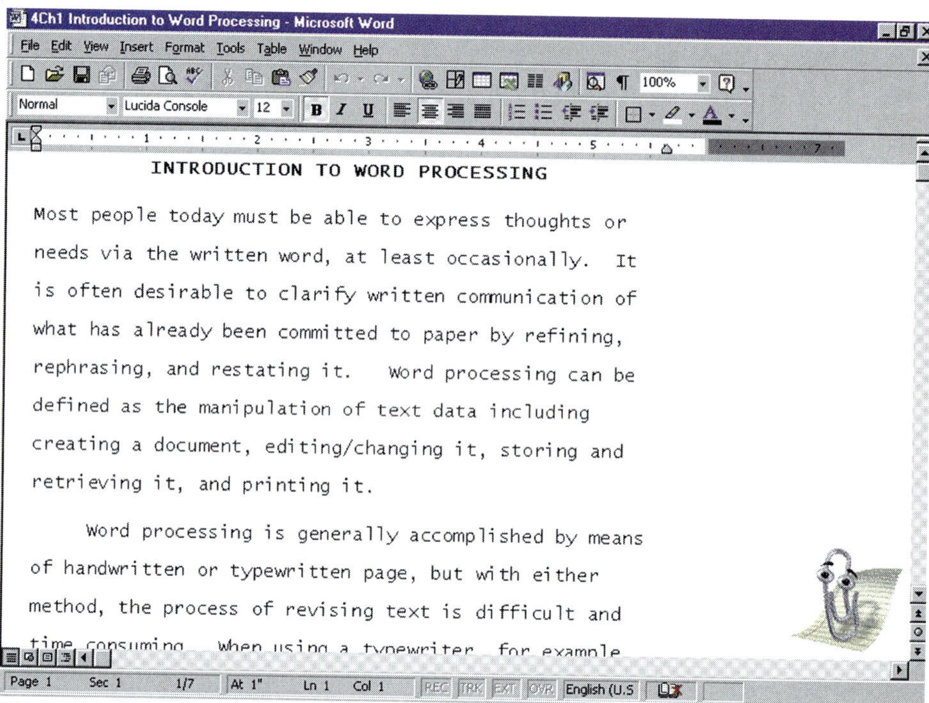

FIGURE 3.10 **The associated 4Ch1 Introduction to Word Processing document displayed using Microsoft Word.**

Click the Close button on the Word title bar to return to the window containing the textbook files.

6. Select a portion of a column of documents.

Point Point to the first document icon in the column. Leave the pointer over the file until the selection appears.

SHIFT Hold down SHIFT.

Point Point to the last file in the column. All the document icons between the selected documents in the column should appear in blue, indicating that they have been selected. Your screen should look something like Figure 3.11 (the objects you select may be different). Note that a listing of all the selected files along with the total storage appears in the left-hand portion of the window.

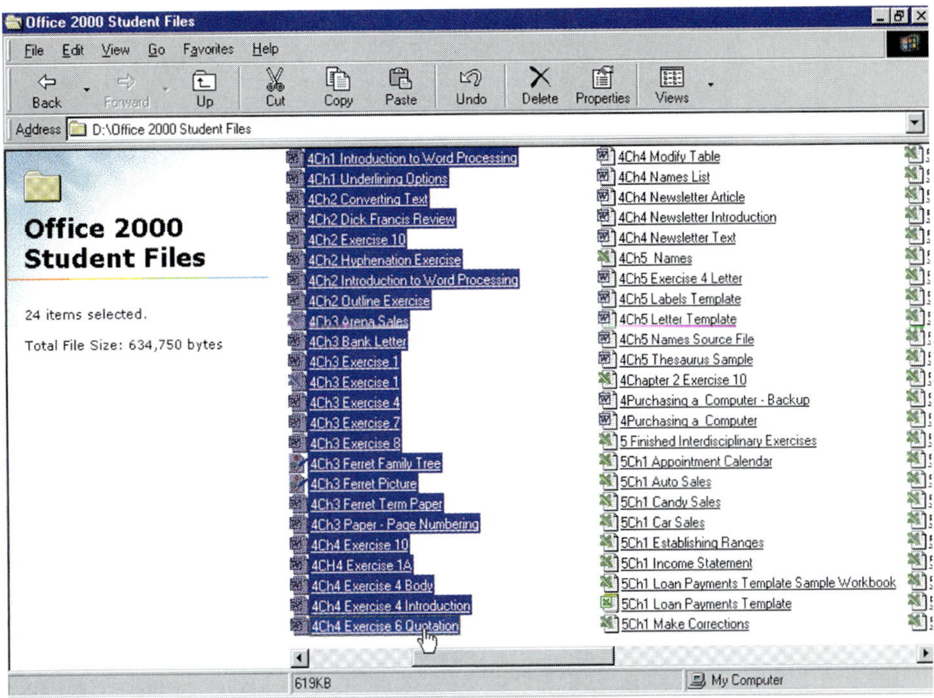

FIGURE 3.11 **Two columns of selected document icons.**

Click Click anywhere in the window to deselect the document icons.

TIMELY TIP

Once you have selected the first document, Windows allows you to position in the window using the scroll bar before selecting the ending file location. If a document in the second column is selected, the display may jump to the right so that the third column is visible.

7. Use a drag operation to include the same files in a selection.

Click and drag Click to the right and just above the document icon in the first column. Drag until the pointer is below and to the right of the last desired icon. The desired icons should be included in the selection, as indicated by the color of the documents included in the selection rectangle (Figure 3.12). When you release the left mouse button, the objects should appear like those shown in Figure 3.13.

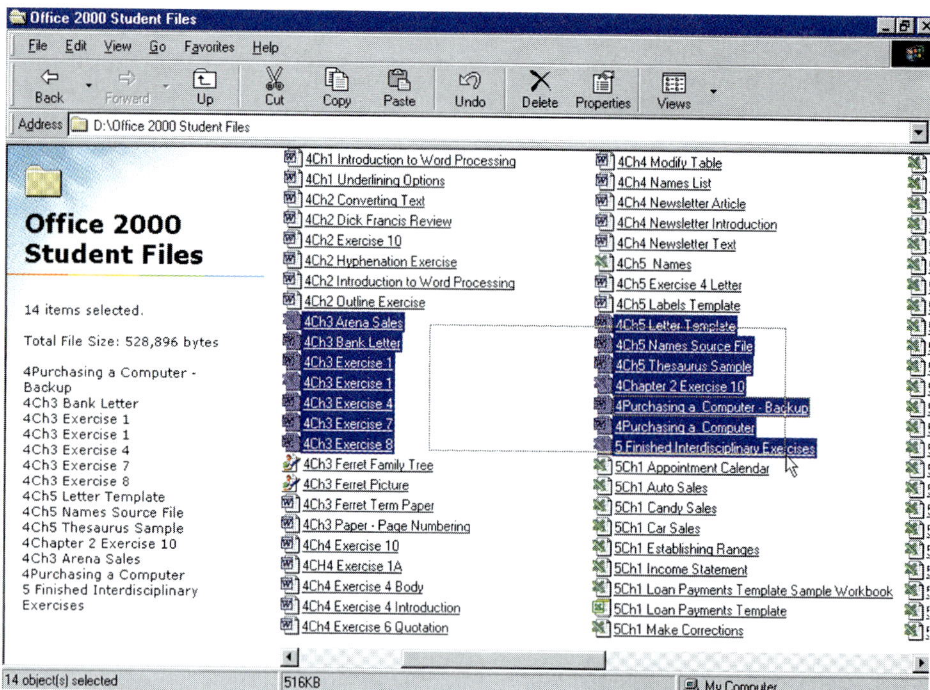

FIGURE 3.12 The selection rectangle includes objects selected in a drag operation.

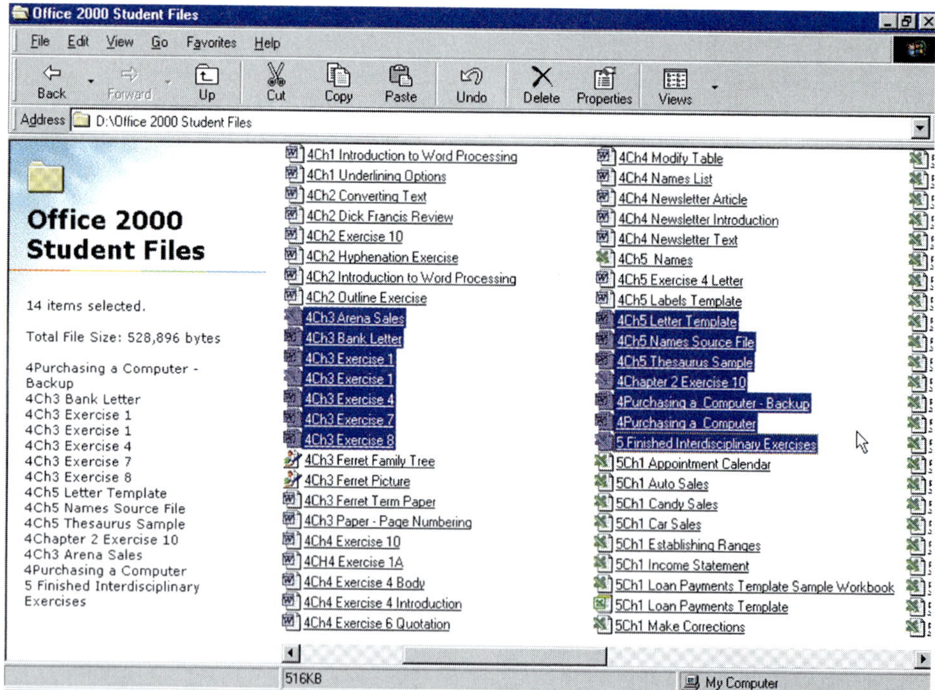

FIGURE 3.13 The selected objects.

Click Click any unused area of the window to cancel the selection.

8. Select every other document icon in the first column.

Point Point the first document icon in any column.

(CTRL)	Hold down (CTRL).
Point	Point to every other document icon to include them in the selection. Your screen should now appear like that shown in Figure 3.14.

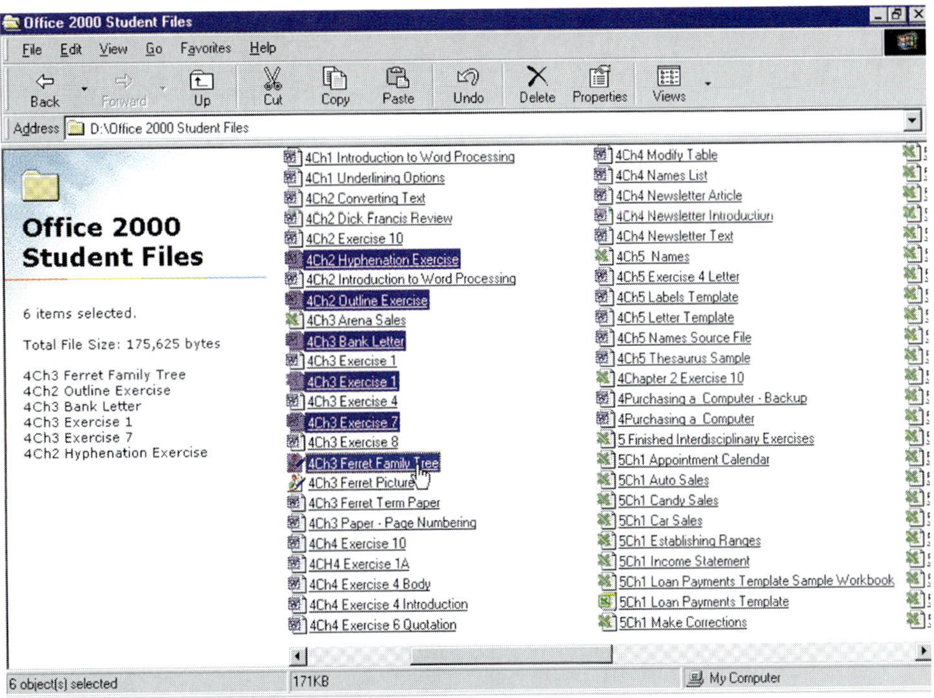

FIGURE 3.14 **Every other object selected in a column.**

Click	Click anywhere in the window to cancel the selection.

9. Click the Restore button of the folder window.

10. Close the folder window.

Reinforcing the Exercise

1. Folders can contain documents or other folders.
2. To select adjacent objects, you click the first object, hold down (SHIFT), and then click the last object.
3. You can also use a drag operation to select adjacent objects.
4. You use (CTRL) in combination with the mouse to select nonadjacent objects.
5. The icon for an associated document includes the icon for the program that was used to create the document.

PERFORMING FILE MAINTENANCE TASKS

The process of file maintenance includes such day-to-day housekeeping tasks as creating new folders; renaming, deleting, moving, or restoring folders and documents; and formatting data disks. These tasks can involve one or more documents.

To perform file maintenance tasks, you use the mouse as the primary input tool. You frequently use the right mouse button to activate the context pop-up menu.

Creating a New Folder

The first step in creating a new folder is right-clicking anywhere in the window accessed using My Computer that will contain the new folder. The context menu opens. You then click the New menu option to open the menu shown in Figure 3.15. When you click the Folder option, a selected (blue) folder icon now appears on-screen (Figure 3.16). The default folder name, New Folder, is highlighted so you can immediately enter a new folder name. That folder is now ready to be used for storing any type of file. (Don't worry about the New Folder icon appearing to cover up other folder icons; if you were to leave this window and then come back to it later, the New Folder icon would appear at the top.)

Folder
Shortcut
Wave Sound
Text Document
bmp Image
Microsoft HTML Document 4.0
Microsoft Access Database
Microsoft Excel Worksheet
Microsoft Word Document
Microsoft Office Binder
Other Office Documents...
Microsoft PowerPoint Presentation
PKZIP File
Image Composer Document
Picture It! Image
Briefcase

FIGURE 3.15 The New menu opens when you choose Folder from the context menu.

Timely Tip

You can also create a new folder by issuing the File, New command sequence.

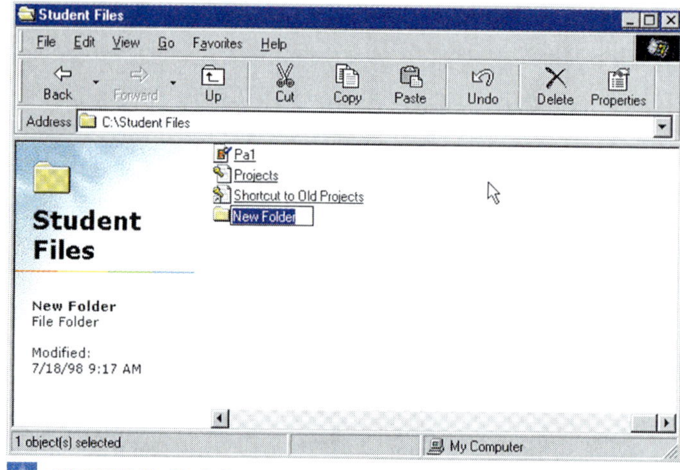

FIGURE 3.16 The newly inserted folder, ready for you to enter a folder name.

Hands-On Exercise: Creating a New Folder

Make certain that you have a data disk in drive A. Using the My Computer window, activate drive A.

1. Create a new folder on drive A.

Right-click Open the context menu by clicking any unused area on the drive A window.

New ▶ Open the New submenu (Figure 3.15). Select the Folder option.

Folder A new folder now appears with the name New Folder (Figure 3.16). The name is highlighted, indicating you can begin typing a new folder name.

Type: `Temporary Folder` Enter the name of the folder.

ENTER Create the file name.

Click Click the folder name to make certain that the folder has been created. It should be empty, like that shown in Figure 3.17.

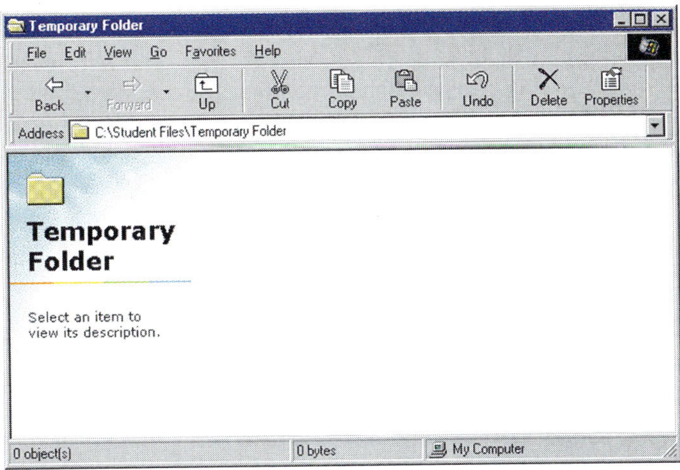

FIGURE 3.17 The newly created, empty Temporary Folder window displayed.

2. Return to the original window.

Click the Back button to return to the original window.

On Your Own

Use the File, New command sequence to add a new folder to the active window.

Reinforcing the Exercise

1. You open a context menu to create a new folder or use the File, New command sequence.
2. The New, Folder command sequence creates a folder with the default name New Folder.
3. You have to enter a name for the created folder, otherwise the default name will be used.
4. Once you have finished entering the new folder name, press Enter to create the folder name.

Copying a Document or Folder

The easiest way to copy a document or folder is to select the desired object and then use the Copy and Paste buttons of the Standard toolbar.

Occasionally you will need to make copies of important documents stored in a folder on the fixed disk and send them to a disk in drive A. A copy of one or more files saved to

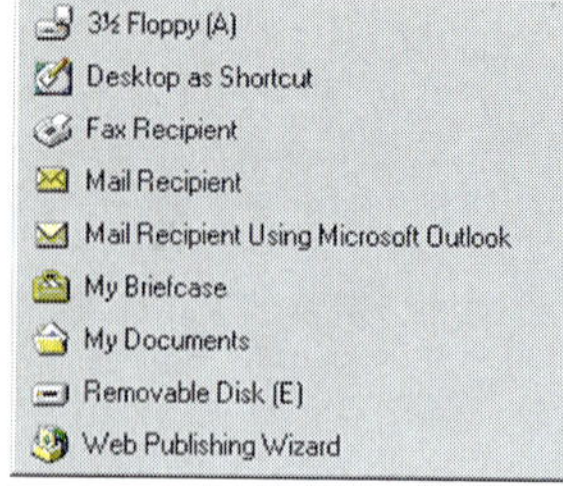

FIGURE 3.18
The Send To menu.

disk is called a **backup**. If you later destroy an important document, you can recreate it by copying the backup copy of the document and storing it in the desired folder; this process is called **recovery**.

Once you have selected documents that you wish to copy to a diskette, you right-click to open the context menu. Select the Send To option to open the menu like that in Figure 3.18. Then select the 3½ Floppy (A) option. The copy window appears (Figure 3.19) and the documents are now copied to the diskette. Be sure to place the diskette with the copied files in a safe place for later use.

If you ever need the backup to recover an important document, use My Computer to open the drive A window, which contains the backup, and the fixed disk window, which contains the folder you want to copy the files to. Use a drag operation to copy the desired documents from the disk to the desired folder on the fixed disk.

If you are copying files from one device or folder to another using the single Web window interface, you position to the device or folder containing the files to be copied, select the files, and then click the Copy button. The files are placed on the clipboard. You now position to the device or folder that is to receive the files and click the Paste button to copy the files from the clipboard to the receiving folder. The files are now placed in the receiving location.

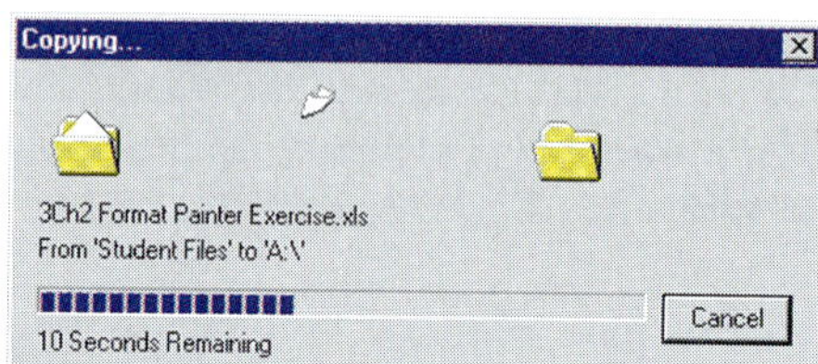

FIGURE 3.19 **The Copy window with status information about the Copy process being performed.**

TIMELY TIP

If you are using the Classic Windows mode and have both the window containing the files to be copied and the window to receive the file visible on the screen, you can use a drag operation to drag the selected files to the receiving window.

If you want to use a drag operation to copy a file from one folder to another on the **same** drive you need to hold down the (CTRL) key while you drag the files. Otherwise the file is just moved, not copied.

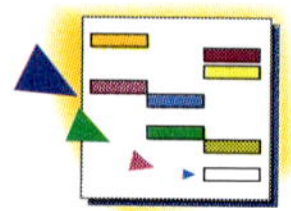

HANDS-ON EXERCISE: COPYING A DOCUMENT

1. Copy a document from the drive A window to the Temporary Folder Window.

3Ch2 Ferret Expo Brochure Point to this document in the window to select it. It should now appear in blue.

(CTRL) **+ Click and drag** While holding down the (CTRL) key, click and drag the document from the drive A window to the Temporary Folder you created earlier. A "phantom" of the icon moves with the operation. When the icon is at the Temporary Folder window, release the mouse button. The copy window with a flying document appears indicating that the document is being copied. When the copy operation is completed, the dialog box disappears, and the document icon appears in both windows. If you don't hold down the CTRL key when you are dragging an item to a location on the same disk, a Move operation will occur instead of a Copy (unless you are selecting a different disk).

2. **Open the Temporary Folder window.** It should look like Figure 3.20.

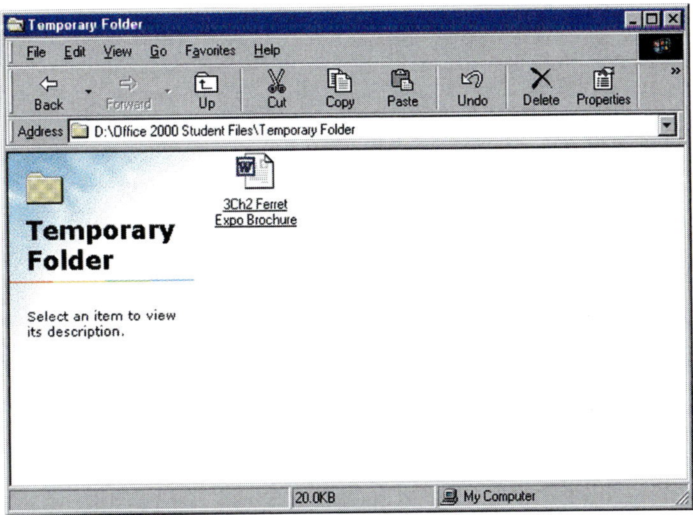

FIGURE 3.20 The Temporary Folder window with the copied file.

3. **Close the Temporary Folder window.**

Return to the original folder.

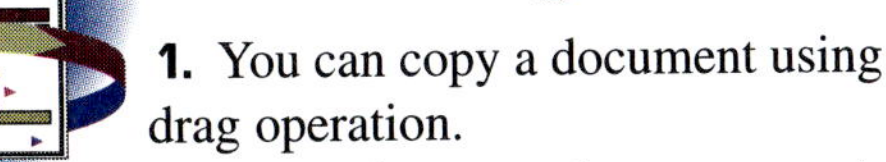

Reinforcing the Exercise

1. You can copy a document using a drag operation.
2. You can also copy documents using the Send To option of the context menu.
3. One or more documents can be copied at a time.
4. Use the Copy command to execute the backup and recovery processes.
5. Use the Copy and Paste buttons to copy files from one folder to another using Web view.

Deleting a Document or Folder

Once you have selected a folder or document, you can delete it by clicking the Delete button or by pressing TAB. A Confirm File Delete dialog box appears (Figure 3.21), asking if you really want to delete the indicated object. Click Yes to delete the document or folder.

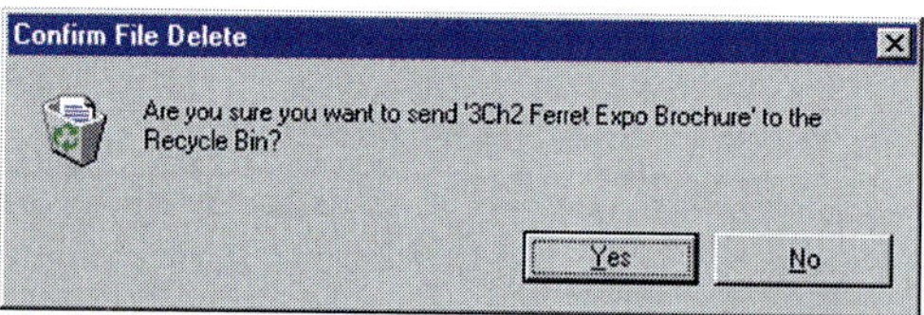

FIGURE 3.21 The Confirm File Delete dialog box is used by Windows to make certain that you want to delete a document or folder.

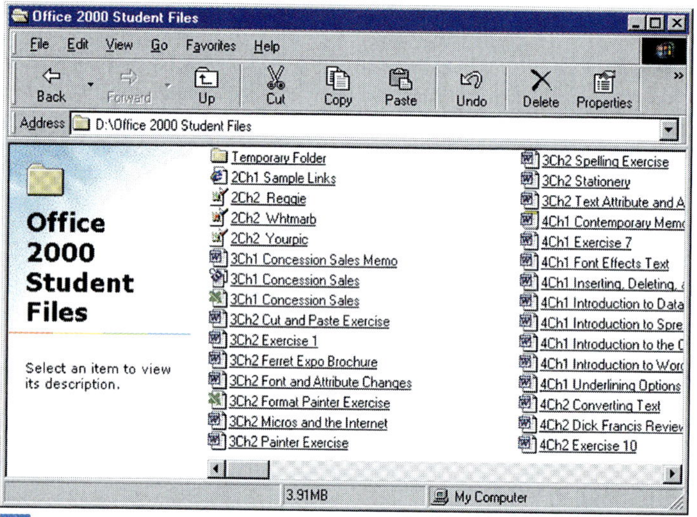

FIGURE 3.22 The Temporary folder in the window.

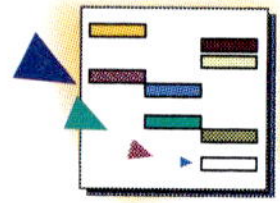

Hands-On Exercise: Deleting the Temporary Folder

1. Delete the contents of the Temporary Folder window shown in Figure 3.22.

Temporary Folder — Click to open the Temporary Folder Window.

3Ch2 Ferret Expo Brochure Point to select the document.

Click the Delete button of the Standard toolbar to open the Confirm File Delete dialog box for the 3Ch2 Ferret Expo Brochure document (Figure 3.21).

Click to delete the file. The file icon should no longer be visible in the Temporary Folder window.

Click to return to the original window.

2. Delete the Temporary Folder.

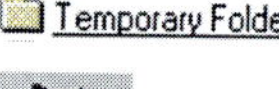

Point to select the Temporary Folder entry.

The Confirm Folder Delete dialog box now appears.

Yes — Click to delete the folder. When the delete operation is finished, the folder is no longer visible in the drive A window.

TIMELY TIP

You can combine the document delete and folder delete operations into one by deleting a folder without concern for how many files it may hold.

3. Close the Window.

Click the Close button on the title bar to return to the desktop.

Reinforcing the Exercise

1. Click the Delete button or Press (DEL) to delete selected documents or folders.
2. You must confirm that you want to delete the selected documents or folders.
3. When you delete a folder that contains several documents, the documents are deleted as well.

USING THE RECYCLE BIN TO UNDELETE A DOCUMENT

You will, from time to time, delete a document that you did not want to delete. Don't despair. When Windows deletes a document, it copies it to the **Recycle Bin** so that it can be reconstructed at a later time. Open the Recycle Bin on the desktop to see a list of all the recently deleted files (Figure 3.23).

FIGURE 3.23 The Recycle Bin dialog box lists the deleted documents.

The easiest way to restore a file is to select the file to be restored, right-click the mouse to activate the context menu, and then select the Restore option. The file is then restored to its original location.

If you want to restore the file to a location different from its original location you must open the window you want to put it in. Once you have located the name of the document you want undeleted, you can use a click and drag operation to place it in the desired window. The file is now restored.

TIMELY TIP

Documents saved to disk in drive A or drive B, not on the fixed drive, are not copied to the Recycle Bin when they are deleted.

RENAMING A DOCUMENT OR FOLDER

An easy way to rename a document or folder is to right-click that object and then select the Rename command from the context menu. The name of the selected object appears in a rectangle that contains the insertion point (Figure 3.24). When you enter the first character of the new name, the old name is erased. Continue to enter the characters of the new name, and then press (ENTER) or click any unused area to rename the object.

FIGURE 3.24
A document icon that is ready to be renamed.

TIMELY TIP

You can use the following procedure to rename a file using Classic Windows mode. Position the pointer on the name, click once, pause, and click again. The name box appears, and you can enter the new object name (Figure 3.24). If you do not have the pointer properly positioned or if you click too quickly the second time, however, a folder may open or an associated application may start running.

PRINTING A DOCUMENT

Windows allows you to print a document that has been associated with a software application. Remember that the icon for an associated document includes the logo of the application to which it is associated. If a document is not associated with an application, the Microsoft flag appears in the icon.

To print an associated document, select the document's icon by clicking it with the mouse, open the File menu from the menu bar, and select the Print command. The associated application is started, the document is loaded, and then it is printed. Once the document has been sent to the printer, you are returned to the window that originally contained that document icon.

VERIFYING THE DOCUMENT TO BE PRINTED

You may not be certain about the contents of a document that you want to print. You can verify a document's contents by selecting it and then issuing the File, Quick View menu command sequence. The Quick View window opens, displaying the contents of the document (Figure 3.25).

The icons at the top of the Quick View window allow you to perform such tasks as opening the file for editing or increasing or decreasing the size of the font used in the window. You can also view other documents by dragging their icons into the Quick View window.

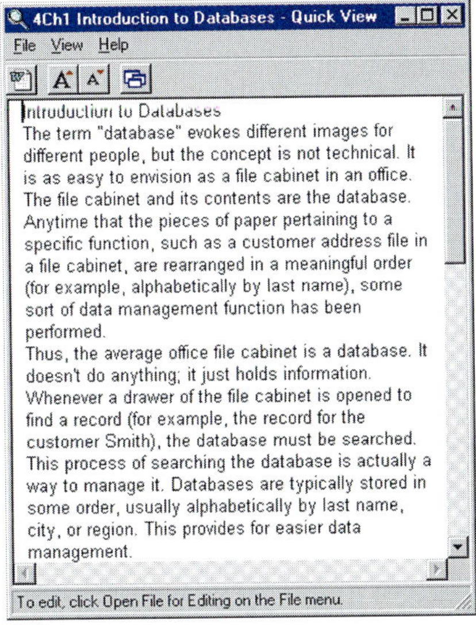

FIGURE 3.25 The Quick View window allows you to verify the contents of a document before printing it.

FORMATTING A DATA DISK

Before you can use a disk in your computer, it must undergo a process called **formatting**. You use the Format command to initialize the disk so it conforms to a recording format that your computer can use. As it executes, the Format command analyzes the entire disk for defective sectors, initializes the directory (the place on the disk where the document names are kept), sets up space for the file allocation table (which keeps track of the storage areas the document uses), and records the boot program in the boot record. (The boot program loads the system files if they are present or indicates that no system files are present if you try to boot with this disk.)

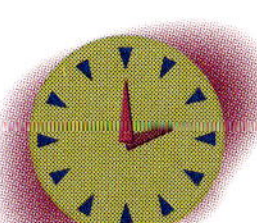

TIMELY TIP

Most computer supply stores sell unformatted and preformatted disks. The preformatted disks typically sell for slightly more than unformatted diskettes, but they can save you the aggravation of sending each disk through the formatting process.

It should be noted that as you use and possibly abuse your disks they can go bad. If you start to get bad sector errors, you might want to try to use some of the third-party utilities that can sometimes successfully be used to "resurrect" your data. If this happens, you should probably copy your files to another disk and then get rid of the offending disk.

You access the Format command from the My Computer window. First place the disk to be formatted in the appropriate drive (typically drive A). In the My Computer window, right-click the icon for the drive containing the disk to be formatted (drive A). Then select the Format command to open the Format dialog box shown in Figure 3.26. Make certain that the appropriate disk type is displayed in the Capacity list box. The Format type box provides three basic methods of formatting a disk (Table 3.1).

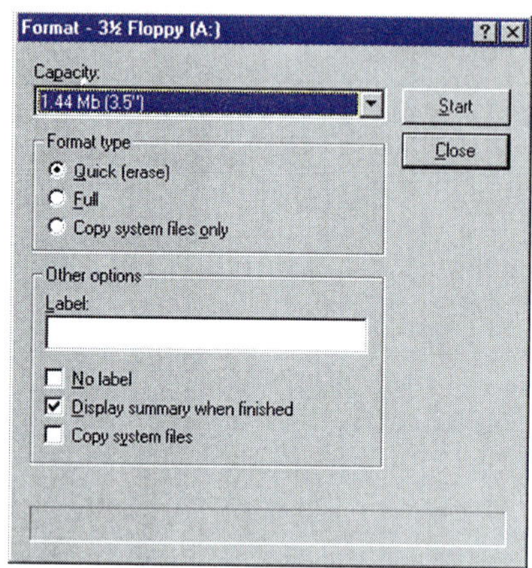

FIGURE 3.26 The Format dialog box controls how a disk is formatted.

TABLE 3.1 Format Types

Option	Task Performed
Quick (erase)	Formats the disk by erasing the files that are present without scanning for bad areas on the disk. It speeds up the formatting process. This option can only be used on disks that have previously been formatted.
Full	Does a complete format of the disk by checking for and marking any bad areas on the disk so that they will not be used later. This option must be used when a disk is formatted for the first time.
Copy system files only	Adds the system files to the disk without formatting so that the disk can be used to start the computer. A disk formatted by this option must be blank. You should always have one of these diskettes available in case your hard disk goes bad and the operating system is not readily available. System disks are usually created when you install Windows 98 as well as when you install anti-virus software. Always keep such a disk handy.

The first two options listed in Table 3.1 are used by most people for preparing disks for use. The third option is typically irrelevant for creating data disks because there is no need to start the computer with a data disk (it boots from the fixed disk). Besides, the system files take up almost 400,000 bytes of disk space.

The Other options box in the Format dialog box provides three options. The Label option lets you specify a label for the disk. Many students place their names here.

The Copy system files option does the same thing as the Copy system files option discussed in Table 3.1.

The Display summary when finished option is selected by default. This option tells the computer to display a report summary (Figure 3.27).

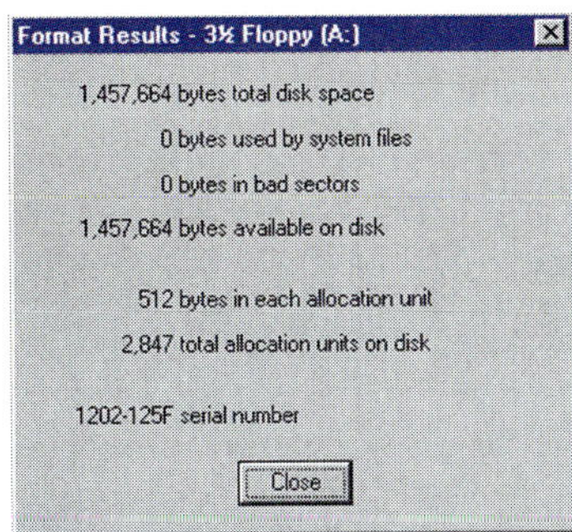

FIGURE 3.27 The Format Results dialog box showing summary information for a disk that has just been formatted.

Once formatting is complete, the system issues a report about the disk in a Format Results dialog box (Figure 3.27). It displays data about the size of the disk and the size of allocation units (sectors). It also displays the volume serial number, which is automatically recorded by Windows and used to identify that specific disk.

During the initial formatting process for a disk, discovery of any defective sectors in a track results in the entire track's being marked as reserved and unavailable for use. This prevents any sectors in the reserved track from being allocated to a data file. Windows reports the total amount of defective space with a screen message (such as "4608 bytes in bad sectors") and subtracts this amount from the total bytes available on the disk (Figure 3.27).

After you have formatted the disk, click the Close button to return to the Format dialog box. If there are no more disks to be formatted, click the Format dialog box's Close button to return to the My Computer window.

Timely Tip

Windows is so careful when it is formatting a disk initially that it is sometimes too conservative when marking bad sectors. If you format a disk and are informed that it contains bad sectors, try formatting again; on the next try, the sectors may be all right after all. Since Windows never uses the bad sectors, it is perfectly OK to keep any disk containing bad sectors and use just as you would any other. However, if bad sectors suddenly start to appear on a disk that you have been using, it is probably best to throw it away after you have copied any files from it.

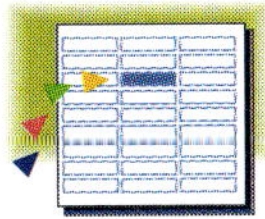

On Your Own

If you own your own computer with Windows 98 installed, you might be interested in a number of System Tools that tend to make life easier for the computer owner. Some of the Systems Tools options you can use are listed below.

- Use the Scheduled Tasks to schedule a task to run when it's most convenient to you.
- Use Disk Defragmenter to make your hard disk more efficient so that programs run faster.
- Use Resource Meter to find out what system resources your programs are using.
- Use System File Checker to verify the integrity of your operating systems files as well as fix any bad files.
- Use the Windows Tune Up to get the best performance from your computer
- Use the System Information option to obtain detailed information about your computer and such things as the amount of RAM and how many resources are being used.

It is also a good idea to run these utilities on a regular schedule of at least once a month. This helps keep your computer system healthy.

USING THE PRINT MANAGER

Printing for all Windows applications is controlled by the **Print Manager**. This means any changes in the printer setup that you make at one location in Windows will affect all Windows application programs. This section introduces you to the Print Manager by showing you how to change the default printer and manipulate the print queue.

CHANGING THE DEFAULT PRINTER

A computer may be connected to more than one printer. The default printer is the one that will print all documents unless Windows is informed otherwise.

To select the default printer, you first enter the command sequence Start, Settings, Printers. In the Printers window that appears (Figure 3.28), click the desired printer. Then issue the command sequence File, Set As Default. The printer you have chosen will be used by all Windows application programs in this and future Windows sessions, until you change the default again. All printing occurs in background mode, which means you can do other tasks while the printing process proceeds.

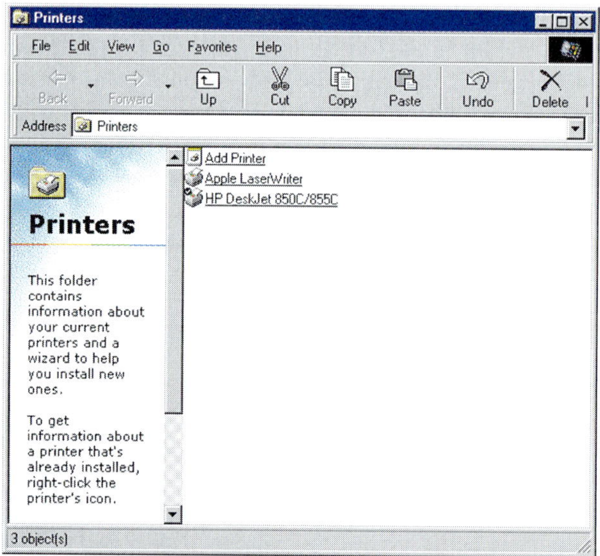

FIGURE 3.28 The Printers window allows you to select the default printer.

CHECKING PRINTER STATUS AND MANAGING THE PRINT QUEUE

The Print Manager icon appears at the bottom of the screen in the status bar when any print operations are being performed. This indicates that the Print Manager is running in **background mode**, printing any jobs that you have sent to the printer. If something goes wrong during a print run (for instance, you receive a message indicating that the printer is not working), a red question mark becomes part of the Print Manager icon. Double-click the icon to display the Print Manager window. For example, the Print Manager window shown in Figure 3.29 indicates that an HP DeskJet printer is currently printing. It displays a list of documents waiting to be printed, called the **print queue**.

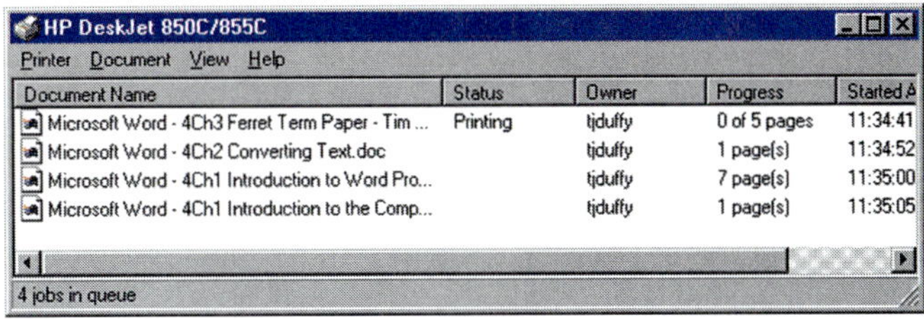

FIGURE 3.29 The Print Manager window for the HP DeskJet printer with several files printing.

To delete a document from the print queue, click the appropriate name in the Document Name list, and then enter the command sequence Document, Cancel. You can also change the position of a document in the print queue by clicking the document name and dragging it to a new location. You cannot move a document in front of a document currently being printed.

On Your Own

Many of the commands covered in this chapter can also be invoked by using the **Explorer** feature of Windows (Figure 3.30). Start Explorer by pointing to the Start button, right-clicking, and selecting the Explore option from the context menu. The Explorer window opens (Figure 3.30). This window has two sections, or panes: the All Folders pane and the Contents pane. These panes display the hierarchy of folders and documents stored on various computer resources. This hierarchy is similar to a tree, with folders and documents branching off from other folders.

With the Explorer window open, try the following tasks:

- In the All Folders pane, click on an **Expand button** (a plus (+) sign to the left of a folder icon).
- Click on a **Collapse button** (a minus (–) sign to the left of a folder icon).
- In the Contents pane, open a context menu.
- Create a new folder. Name it.
- Copy a document to the new folder.
- Rename the folder.
- Delete the new folder.
- Close Explorer.

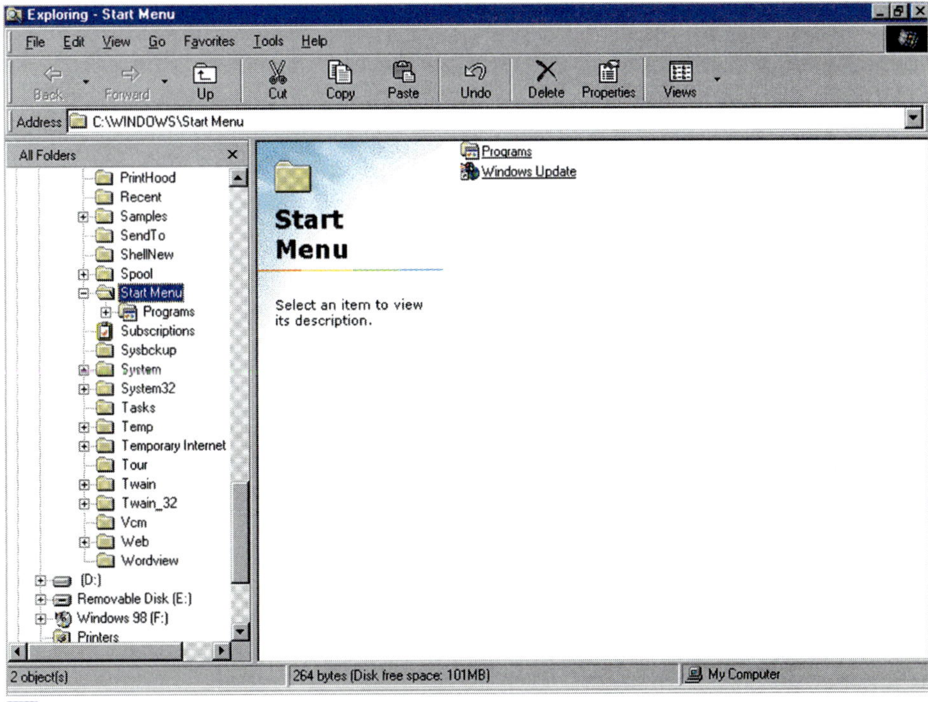

FIGURE 3.30 The Explorer window.

Session Review

Windows 98 provides a file maintenance system that allows you to manipulate items you have saved to disk.

Windows uses a folder metaphor to describe its file maintenance system. Documents (files) are stored in folders. Folders can be nested in one another; that is, a folder can have several different levels of folders. A folder can contain such things as part of the operating system, a workbook, and a word processing document.

Before you can work with documents and folders, you must select them. You select a single document or folder by clicking the desired object. To select multiple adjacent objects, you drag the pointer over the desired objects, or hold down (SHIFT) and then click the first and last objects. Select multiple nonadjacent objects by holding down (CTRL) and clicking the desired objects.

When you double-click an associated file, the application program that was used to create that object automatically starts.

File maintenance tasks include creating new folders, renaming existing objects, copying objects from one location to another, deleting an object from disk, or restoring an object using the Recycle Bin.

Windows provides several methods for formatting a disk. Any disk must be formatted at least once. Two of the formatting methods are commonly used for preparing data disks for use.

The Explorer feature of Windows provides much of the same information as the My Computer window, but the Explorer window presents two panes of data. The left-most pane, labeled All Folders, shows the hierarchy of the folders using a tree structure. To expand the tree, you click a button with a plus sign (+), called an Expand button, which appears to the left of a folder name. To reduce the tree, you click a button with a minus sign (–), called a Collapse button. The right-most pane in the Explorer window, labeled Contents, shows the contents of the selected folder or drive.

The Print Manager controls how files are printed. All print operations using Windows go through the Print Manager. You can use the Print Manager to cancel print operations that have already been started by a Windows application program.

Key Terms and Concepts

Session Quiz

Multiple Choice

1. Which of the following do you use to select multiple adjacent objects?
   - **a.** (SHIFT)
   - **b.** (CTRL)
   - **c.** a drag operation
   - **d.** all of the above
2. Which of the following statements about Explorer is/are false?
   - **a.** It allows you to delete documents.
   - **b.** It allows you to control which types of documents and folders are listed.
   - **c.** It lists only one folder or disk device at a time.
   - **d.** It allows you to specify more than one object.

3. Which of the following statements is false regarding folders and the My Computer window?
   a. You can rename a folder.
   b. You can delete a folder.
   c. You can create a folder.
   d. You can print a document.
   e. None of the above.
4. Which of the following options of the Format dialog box cannot be used on a disk?
   a. Label
   b. Copy system files
   c. Quick (erase)
   d. Copy directory
5. How do you alter the position of a document in the Print Manager print queue?
   a. Select the Priority command and select the next document.
   b. Select the Rush command from the Options menu.
   c. Click the desired document and drag it to the new location in the print queue.
   d. None of the above.

True/False

6. The drive icons allow you to control which folders and files are displayed using Explorer.
7. When specifying multiple objects for an operation, you can specify only adjacent object names.
8. You can restore deleted files using the Recycle Bin.
9. Before you can open an associated document, you must start the related application program.
10. The Print Manager controls the printing of any Windows application program.

Session Review Exercises

1. Define the following terms:
   a. Print Manager
   b. print queue
   c. Recycle Bin
   d. associated file
2. When you double-click a(n) ____________ document, the application program automatically starts, and then the document opens.
3. The ____________ command is used to prepare a disk for use by the computer.
4. Folders are created using the ____________ command of the context menu.
5. Folders are erased by pressing the ____________ key.
6. Folders and documents can be renamed using the ____________ command from the context menu.
7. The File ____________ command can only be used with associated documents.
8. The Recycle Bin lets you restore a document from the fixed disk but does not let you restore a file that was erased from a ____________.
9. The ____________ pane of the Explorer contains a list of the folders and documents in the selected drive or folder.
10. In the Explorer Window, a folder icon with a ____________ sign has no branch folders.
11. You must hold down the ____________ key when you are using the mouse to select multiple nonadjacent documents or folders.
12. The process of copying files to a disk to protect the original files is called ____________.
13. You can select multiple adjacent documents by holding down the ____________ key.
14. You can also select multiple adjacent documents by using a ____________ operation.
15. A selected document or folder appears ____________ in a different color.
16. To see the contents of a document before printing, you must use the ____________ ____________ command.
17. A document in the Recycle Bin can be restored by ____________ it to its original window.
18. A document name can contain up to ____________ characters.
19. The process of fixing a damaged or deleted file by copying a file to the fixed disk is called ____________.
20. You can delete a ____________ or document by using DEL.

Computer Exercises

1. Use the Format command to format any disks that you will be using this school term. Be sure to format them as data disks. You do not want the system files on any of these disks.
2. Create the folder structure shown in Figure 3.31. This exercise reinforces the folder concepts introduced in this chapter. It requires that you have the student data disk used with this text in drive A.

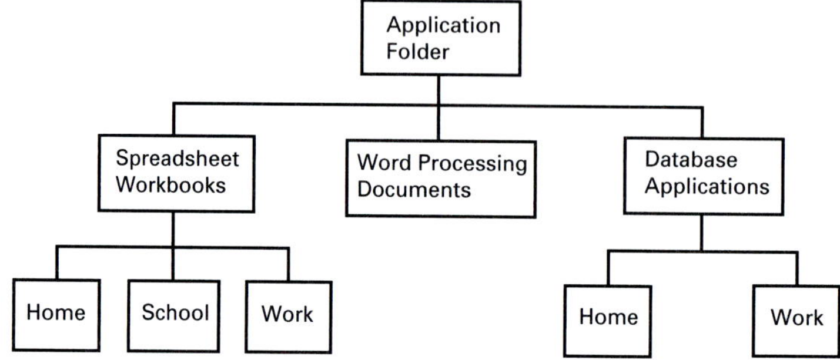

FIGURE 3.31 The hierarchy of the folder structure to be created.

After you have built the new folders, start Explorer. Expand all of the folders. Your Explorer window should look like that shown in Figure 3.32. Once you complete this exercise, delete all folders.

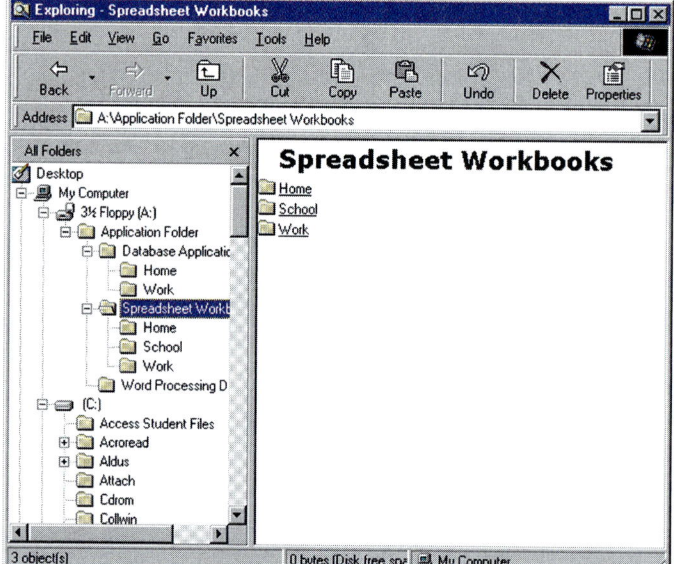

FIGURE 3.32 The newly created folders shown in expanded format by using the Explorer window.

3. This exercise reinforces the use of the New and Copy commands. It requires you to open the disk area that contains your textbook-related documents.
   a. Create a new folder and name it Temporary Storage Area.
   b. Copy the following documents to it: 4Ch1 Introduction to Spreadsheets, 4Ch1 Introduction to the Computer, and 4Ch1 Introduction to Databases.
   c. Open the Temporary Storage Area folder to verify that the documents were copied correctly.
   d. Close the Temporary Storage Area folder.
   e. Delete the Temporary Storage Area folder.
4. Double-click the 4Ch1 Introduction to Databases associated document. The document should be loaded automatically by Word. Click the Close button of the Word window to return to the desktop.

5. Select the 4Ch1 Introduction to Spreadsheets document. Issue a File, Quick View command sequence. Your screen should now appear like that shown in Figure 3.33.
   a. Use the scroll bar to examine the document.
   b. Click the Open file for editing button. Word should now be started, and the document opened.
   c. Click the Close button of the Word window to return to the desktop.

FIGURE 3.33
The 4Ch1 Introduction to Spreadsheets document displayed in the Quick View window.

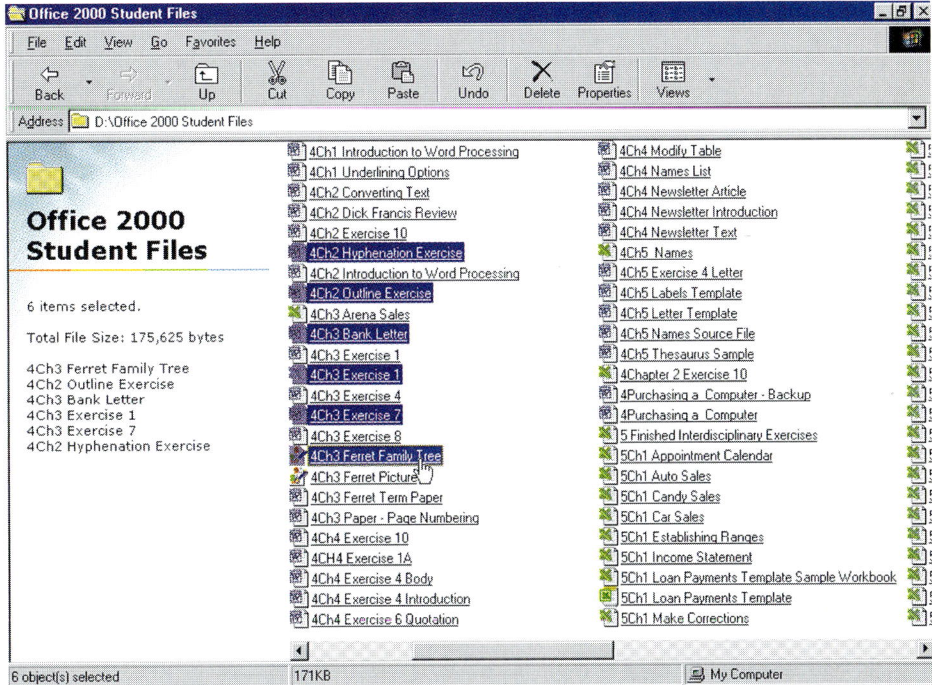

6. Select the 4Ch1 Introduction to Databases document.
   a. Issue the File, Print command sequence.
   b. The document should begin printing.
   c. After the document is printed, you should be returned to the desktop.
   d. If the printer icon is visible in the lower-right corner of your screen, double-click it to invoke the Print Manager. Examine the window and the status of the print process.
   e. Click the Close button of the Print Manager window to return to the desktop.
7. Use the Explorer feature of Windows to examine the device and/or folder used for storing your textbook documents.
8. Experiment with selecting multiple documents by using the mouse.
   a. Select adjacent documents by using a drag operation.
   b. Select adjacent documents by using (SHIFT).
   c. Select nonadjacent documents by using (CTRL).
9. Activate the Recyle Bin to see if there are any documents that you can restore. If possible, restore one of the documents that you have erased previously (remember, if your original files resided on drive A, they cannot be restored using the Recycle Bin).
10. Use the Start, Printers Setting command sequence to see if there are any other printers that you can use with your Windows installation. Close the window when you are finished.

Glossary

Active Desktop The name now used by Windows to refer to the desktop.

active window The window that appears on top when multiple windows are open on the desktop. Any commands you issue or text you enter affects only the active window.

associated document A document that has been saved to disk by a specific software application and is represented in a folder by an icon with an application logo on it. When you select an associated document, the application that was used to create that document is started and the document is loaded.

background mode The Print Manager can run printing jobs as you complete other tasks. During background mode, the Print Manager icon appears in the status bar, and if something goes wrong during a print job, a red question mark becomes part of the Print Manager icon.

backup A copy of one or more files saved to disk.

binder Holds copies of related electronic documents you have created in various Office applications. You can save, move, and print a binder as you would a single document. Changes that you make to the copy of the document that is in a binder are reflected in the original document.

border 1. A box or line surrounding a block of text. 2. Contains the labels of the worksheet's rows and columns. 3. The edge of a window. When you position the pointer on the border, the pointer changes to a double-headed arrow, which allows you to resize the window.

check box Turns an option on and off.

click To quickly press and release the left mouse button; done to select an object.

clipboard An area in memory used to store data temporarily during a cut, paste, or copy operation. The clipboard can store data only for one Cut or Copy command; the data in the clipboard is destroyed and replaced when a subsequent Cut or Copy command is issued.

Clipboard Viewer Used to see just exactly what resides in the Clipboard once you have copied information to the Clipboard.

Close button The rightmost button on the title bar, used to close a window or application.

Collapse button In the All Folders pane of Explorer, you click this button to close a folder and hide its contents.

command button In an open dialog box, you click this button to issue commands.

command sequence A series of menu selections. For example, to issue the File, Open command sequence, you choose File from the menu bar and then choose Open from the File menu.

Contents tab Used to locate information on general topics.

context menu This menu shows the most frequently used commands for the specific object.

control Object within a dialog box, such as a text box, list box, check box, or command button.

control-menu button Located at the far left end of a window's title bar, this button is a throwback to older versions of Windows and is now rarely used.

Copy command Occurs when a likeness of data is placed in the Clipboard, leaving the original data unchanged.

Cut command Removes the data from its original location and places it in the Clipboard.

deselect To reverse the action of selecting an object by clicking anywhere outside the selected object.

desktop An on-screen workspace on which you can perform a variety of tasks by clicking buttons or icons that represent applications, commands, or files.

dialog box A type of window that prompts you for information needed to carry out a command. A dialog box opens when you select a menu option that has an ellipsis after its name or when you click certain buttons.

disk operating system (DOS) A set of programs that allows you to interact with the computer.

document Represents stored data that can be processed by an application program or by the computer itself.

double-click To press and release the left mouse button twice in rapid succession.

drag To press and hold the left mouse button while moving the mouse; done to select multiple lines or to move an object to another location.

ellipsis A dialog box appears when you choose a menu option that has an ellipsis.

Expand button In the All Folders pane of Explorer, you click this button to open a folder and display its contents.

Explorer A feature of Windows 95 that displays the hierarchy of folders and documents stored on various computer resources. Using Explorer, you can execute many file maintenance commands.

file Computer term, rather than a Windows-related term, for a document.

file maintenance The process of interacting with objects that you have saved to disk.

folder In Windows' file maintenance system, the storage place for documents or other folders.

formatting The process of initializing a disk so it conforms to a recording format that your computer can use. The formatting process includes analyzing the disk for defective sectors, initializing the directory, setting up space for the allocation table, and recording the boot program.

graphical user interface (GUI) A software program that allows you to communicate with your computer by using a pointing device called a mouse. This tool for executing commands is quicker than a text-based environment, in which you execute commands by entering keystrokes.

Help feature A Windows feature that provides information on all desktop objects.

icon A graphic representation of an object on the desktop.

Iinactive window Any window that appears beneath the active window. You can click anywhere on an inactive window to make it the active window.

Index tab Used to locate information using keywords.

Internet Explorer Channel Bar Provides access to a number of Web sites via your Web browser.

keyboard shortcut command An alternate command to type to select a menu option.

list box Displays a list of options from which you can choose.

Maximize button Click this button to enlarge a window so it fills the entire screen.

menu bar Located under the title bar in a window, the menu bar contains the names of menus you can open to access commands. Windows is consistent in how menus are arranged from application to application, making it easy to learn various Windows applications.

Minimize button Click this button to take the window off the desktop and place a button for it on the taskbar.

mouse A pointing device used in conjunction with a graphic user interface to execute commands quickly and easily.

multitasking Windows capability to run multiple applications at one time.

My Computer The icon that opens a window that displays information about the resources of your computer, such as printers, the disk drive(s), fixed disk(s), and the CD-ROM drive, if any.

object 1. A PowerPoint entity such as a text block, chart, table, or organization chart. You enter the text of a slide inside a text object. 2. An entity that is controlled by Visual Basic and, in turn, controls anything created by Excel or any way Excel functions. Excel objects include workbooks, worksheets, charts, ranges, dialog boxes, and menu items. 3. Any item that appears on the desktop, such as a document, a field in a database, or a button on a toolbar.

Online Layout view Divides the screen into two panes: The left pane lists the elements of the document, such as section headings and table headings. The right pane displays the complete text of the document. The item selected in the left pane is the item displayed at the top of the right pane. This view is particularly good to use with long documents.

operating system A complex set of computer instructions that comes between you and your computer. It accepts a command from the user, evaluates that command, and then executes it.

option button Turns options on or off.

Outlook Express The icon that allows you to access Microsoft's E-mail software.

Paint program A built-in program contained in Windows that allows you to do freehand drawing.

Paste command Copies data from the Clipboard and places it in a document.

point 1. The unit of measure of a font. An inch consists of 72 points. 2. To move the mouse so that the pointer rests on an object.

Print Manager Controls all printing operations for Windows.

print queue A list of documents waiting to be printed displayed in the Print Manager window.tion or object is displayed.

property Controls how an object behaves and operates in a Windows environment. An object can have several properties, and you control the properties of an object by entering values in a properties sheet.

pull-down menu A menu opened from the menu bar.

recovery The process of recreating a lost or damaged document by copying the backup copy.

Recycle Bin A storage area for deleted documents. You can recover a document from the Recycle Bin and put it back in a folder so you can work on it.

resize a window Performed by using a drag operation on the window border.

Restore button Replaces the Maximize button on a window that you have maximized. Click this button to return a window to the size it was before you clicked the Maximize button.

right-click To press the right mouse button; done to open a context menu.

ScreenTip A text box that appears when you click the What's this? button and then click an object. The ScreenTip provides more detailed information on the function of the object than the ToolTip.

scroll bar Located on the right border of a window and contains a scroll box and up and down arrow buttons. Click the up or down arrow button to move up or down the screen one line at a time.

scroll box Part of the scroll bar. You can drag the scroll box up or down to move quickly from one part of a document to another. The position of the scroll box indicates the location of the cursor in the displayed text.

Search tab Used to search for text related to a topic of interest.

select adjacent objects Accomplished in two ways: You can click the first object, hold down M, and then click the last object; all objects between the two clicked objects are included in the selection. You can also use a drag operation: click the first object and drag the pointer to include the last object.

select nonadjacent objects Hold down c as you click the objects.

shortcut command A command entered from the keyboard.

size grip Located in the lower-right corner of a window. When you position the pointer on a size grip, the pointer changes to a double-headed arrow. You can then resize the window by using a drag operation.

spin box A control with a number and small up and down arrow icons to the right of the box.

status area/system tray Located at the far right end of the taskbar, this area displays miniature icons representing small programs that are always in memory.

status bar Located at the bottom of the window, the status bar provides information on an object from the desktop that you select.

taskbar The gray bar that always appears at the bottom of the Windows desktop and contains the Start button and application buttons representing currently open applications or windows.

text box Allows you to enter and edit information that is needed to perform a task, such as entering the name of a file.

title bar Colored bar at the top of a window that contains the name of the open application and four buttons you can use to control the window: the control-menu, Minimize, Maximize (or Restore), and Close buttons.

toolbar The row of buttons that appears below the menu bar in an application window.

ToolTip A small text box that appears when you position the pointer on an object and let it rest there a while. The ToolTip provides information on the function of the object.

What's this button Contains a question mark (?) and usually appears at the top of the open window or dialog box.

WYSIWYG Stands for "what you see is what you get" and refers to the Windows method of displaying text onscreen exactly as it will print to paper.

INDEX